Teacher-to-Teacher Series

student PORTFOLIOS

62279

62279

An NEA Professional Library Publication

Printing History
First Printing: July 1993
Second Printing: December 1993
Third Printing: July 1994

NOTE: The opinions expressed in this book should not be construed as representing the policy or position of the National Education Association. Materials published by the NEA Professional Library are intended to be discussion documents for educators who are concerned with specialized interests of the profession.

Library of Congress Cataloging-in-Publication Data
Student portfolios / (Laura Grosvenor ... et al.).
p. cm. — (Teacher to teacher series)
Includes bibliographical references.
ISBN 0-8106-2901-1
1. Portfolios in education—United States—Case studies.
2. Students—United States—Rating of—Case studies.
3. Teaching—Aides and devices.
4. Education, Elementary —United States.
5. Education, Secondary—United States.

I. Grosvenor, Laura. II. Series.
LB1029.P67S78 1993
371.2'7—dc20   ® GCIU ®©   93-13849

Contents

How to Use this Book

S tudent Portfolios is no ordinary book. It is part of the NEA Professional Library's new Teacher-to-Teacher book series in which classroom teachers speak directly and candidly to other teachers – like you – about their school restructuring efforts.

Printed in the upper righthand corner of every book cover in the series is a routing slip that encourages you to pass the book on to colleagues once you have read it – in other words, to spread the word about school change.

Book topics cover areas such as student assessment, time management, cross-age grouping, and integrating students with special needs into the regular classroom.

Read the Six Stories

Inside each book you will find stories from six or more teachers across the country who discuss, step by step, how they tackled a specific restructuring challenge. They will describe what worked and didn't work, and provide you with any diagrams, checklists, or tables they think other teachers would find useful.

Write Your Own Ideas in the Book

At the end of each story in a book is an area called Personal Reflections. This area is for you and any colleague who reads the story to write related insights and action points for your school or school district to consider.

You see, the purpose of Teacher-to-Teacher books is not only to spread the word about school change but to encourage other teachers to participate in its exploration.

Discuss Your Thoughts With Others

Once you have routed a book through your school, you can meet with colleagues who contributed to the Reader Reflections sections and expand upon your thoughts.

Go Online

Believe it or not, the communication and sharing doesn't have to stop there. If you would like to discuss a Teacher-to-Teacher book topic with teachers across the country, you can. Any NEA member who subscribes to the America Online electronic network can participate in an ongoing forum on Teacher-to-Teacher book topics.

The National Education Association's area on the network is called NEA Online. Once signed on to NEA Online, just keyword to "NEA Prof Library." To subscribe to NEA Online, call 1-800-827-6364, ext. 8544.

Introduction

Call it restructuring,
Call it taking risks,
We, as teachers,
stuck out our necks
To change what we
felt needed changing.
    Laura Grosvenor
    Fourth Grade Teacher

The six stories in this book are about teachers who dared to do just that, to stick out their necks for change. In this case, the change was student-assessment practice, and it was no small undertaking.

After all, there were (and still are) few alternative models to follow, few tried and true strategies to implement. The teachers who tell their stories in this book had agreed, independent of one another, to enter unknown territory. Tradi-tion, time, money, administrators, and parents were not always on their side.

But the teachers perse-vered because as Cheryl Polakowski, a kinder-garten teacher from Kendall Park, New Jersey, put it: "Some of us were no longer willing to assess youngsters on useless, predetermined matters and in ways that had no application to how we were teaching in our classrooms."

Choosing Portfolios

After making the deci-sion to explore alterna-tive assessment prac-tices, the teachers in this book started off in the same direction — toward portfolio assessment.

Their official defini-tions of this venture var-ied a bit, but their per-ceptions seemed to share three essential character-istics. Their portfolios were to be collections of student work that were: (1) longitudinal in na-ture, (2) diverse in con-tent, and (3) collabora-tive in their selection and evaluation. They would also emphasize strengths, development of skills, improvement, and personal reflections and expectations.

These teachers expect-ed portfolios to provide a broader picture of a student's achievement by showing the unfold-ing of skills over time, something a one-time performance on a test cannot possibly do. They also expected portfolios to encourage students to take partial responsibili-ty (through selection and reflection) for their own learning.

Branching Out

The teachers may have started down the same alternative road, but as their stories reveal, they soon branched out onto very different paths.

Process-Folios:

In the Seattle School District, Washington, classroom teachers team-ed up with administra-tors to design portfolios that encouraged students of all grade levels to fo-cus and reflect on their own learning process.

Three-Way Collaborations:

Teachers at Amanda Arnold Elementary, Manhattan, Kansas, centered their approach on a three-way collaboration in which students conduct their own portfolio conferences with their teacher and parent(s).

Early Literacy Assessors:

In South Brunswick Township, New Jersey, early childhood educators worked closely with researchers from Educational Testing Service to create a highly reliable portfolio system for assessing the literacy progress of every child in the district's kindergarten through second grade classes.

Writing Portfolios:

Teachers at Danville High School, Danville, Kentucky, designed a system of across-the-curriculum writing portfolios that meets the new state assessment mandate of the Kentucky Educational Reform Act and has greatly increased student performance in writing.

Schoolwide Portfolios:

While portfolio pioneers in some schools focused on literacy or writing, teachers at Metro High School, Cedar Rapids, Iowa, decided to incorporate all curriculum areas. Today, teachers throughout the school work with students to develop these diverse collections of work.

Video Portfolios:

Six years ago, a teleproductions teacher at Ravenna High School, Ravenna, Ohio, decided to use video portfolios to assess student progress in his electives course. His system is still going strong, yet continually developing.

Final Impressions

The six stories in this book merely scratch the surface of portfolio assessment's vast potential. Collectively, however, they suggest three universal truths about portfolio use.

First, there is not just one "right way" to implement portfolios. All of the teachers in this book have developed successful yet extremely varied approaches.

Second, assessment is integrally tied to teaching strategies, and if assessments change, so must instruction. Laura Grosvenor from Seattle, Washington, exemplifies this point when she says in her story: "Because portfolios are a shared process, there is no longer the 'I teach; you learn' approach to my instruction."

Finally, portfolio use is a slow and evolving process. The storytellers in this book, some of whom have been experimenting with portfolios for more than six years, all claim their stories have not yet ended. They say they will continue to revise their approaches based on future experiences with portfolios.

Perhaps they will discover enough new insights to write *Student Portfolios II!*

– Mary Dalheim
Series Editor

Notes:

_____

_____

_____

_____

Taking ASSESSMENT MATTERS Into Our Own Hands

In October of 1989, I had the pleasure of traveling with my principal, Vicki Foreman, and two other classroom teachers, Jan Perry and Jane McLane, to Washington, D.C. to participate in the second Annual Mastery in Learning Project Conference, sponsored by the National Education Association's National Center for Innovation. At that conference two things occurred that radically altered my way of thinking. First, I had the opportunity to talk with teachers from around the country who were interested in "transforming" their schools into, as researcher Art Costa puts it, "homes for the mind." Secondly, a group of teachers from White Rock, and Gorham, Massachusetts, spoke about some new and different ways in which they were attempting to assess and evaluate students.

The Massachusetts teachers made a particular impression. I was struck by their level of energy. And when they talked about a day when they hoped to be able to present each of their students with a CD ROM portfolio of their K-12 work along with their diploma at graduation, I was awestruck. They talked of the ability to scan student artwork, collect word-processed stories, make audio and video recordings of student readings, even take zap shot photos of students' three-dimensional artwork – and then save it all in computer portfolios that could be used to assess and cultivate student learning.

I returned home to Kimball Elementary School in Seattle, Washington, full of the energy and enthusiasm I had seen and interested in the

LAURA GROSVENOR

Fourth Grade Teacher
Kimball Elementary School
Seattle, Washington

"hows" of using portfolios. I shared my experience the next week at a site coordinators' meeting for the Seattle Schools for the 21st Century and again saw teachers' eyes light up as they saw the potential for such a plan.

Organizing an Assessment Group Of Our Own

Our district had been looking at the issue of alternative assessment, but

To "do portfolios" means to look at instruction and time differently.

no one had told the teachers. What little we knew of alternative assessment, we had read in magazines and professional journals. After a core group of teachers expressed continued interest, Lois Sax, a Chapter 1 teacher, and education consultant David Florio of the Matsushita Foundation suggested that we organize our own group of district teachers to explore the issues of alternative assessment, and of portfolios in particular. The Matsushita group provided some resources and enabled a few of the participants to travel to San Diego, California, and Santa Fe, New Mexico, to see what teachers were doing there.

For the first year, this small group met after school to try to develop a new approach to assessment. Group members were particularly concerned about the district's heavy reliance on CAT (California Achievement Test) scores as a measure of student achievement.

The first months were spent in discussion, sharing, and trying to define what we really wanted to come out of our meetings. We took a particular interest in developing portfolios to assess reading comprehension (we thought that perhaps portfolios could become an alternative to CATs). However, toward the end of the first year, we had found that dealing with reading comprehension in isolation was too limiting and decided that we really wanted to incorporate writing into our portfolio approach.

Sheila Valencia from the University of Washington, a noted authority on portfolios and alternative assessments, attended this ad hoc committee when possible (as a volunteer) and served as a mentor and critical friend.

Joining Forces With Administrators

In December of 1990, the Curriculum Department of the Seattle Public Schools, under the guidance of Elaine Aoki (Head of Language Arts Curriculum) suggested we consolidate several different committees that were all pursuing an interest in alternative assessment. This was a first for Seattle in that administrators, K-12 teachers, and educators from special testing, bilingual, and resource programs all began working together as a team to *explore* an issue.

As with many large district committees, we were short on resources. Sheila Valencia was interested in following through with the group, and so she and Elaine designed a reciprocal teaching arrangement between the University of Washington and Seattle Public Schools. This gave Sheila the time she needed to work closely with us.

The teachers who had been meeting the previous year formed the core of the group and were able to share their stories, questions, and research with the newer members. The team was given one release day a month for the rest of the school year (paid for by the curriculum department) to work on the issues of portfolios and assessment in all curriculum areas. The district had chosen to invest in our work, and by so doing, gave us a certain level of validation.

While administrators or specialists often carry the most weight in committee meetings, the following responsibilities set by this group emphasized active participation by all members, especially the classroom teachers.

1. Attend and Participate in Monthly Meetings

This includes suggesting activities and agenda items for each meeting. These meetings will involve a combination of sharing concerns and ideas, working on new assessments, and providing input on new assessment ideas. Bring samples of new ideas you've tried out to be placed in our resource files.

2. Keep Portfolios

If you teach in a self-contained classroom, keep a portfolio for each of your students; if you teach several classes of students, keep a portfolio for each student in only one of your class periods.

3. Determine Contents, Etc.

The contents and management of the portfolios will be determined at our first meeting. Portfolios should be accessible to students during the regular school day. Do not keep any confidential information in these portfolios. (This issue, in and of itself, turned out to be a six-month exploration and the most important issue for our group.)

4. Keep a Journal

Keep a journal, with at least one entry per week, in which you reflect on and document your experiences with keeping literary portfolios. These can include facts, opinions, feelings, notes for future plans, reminders to yourself, and conversations you've had with others. The purpose of this jour-

Tips **PORTFOLIO MAINTENANCE**

- Be sure that all pieces are dated.

- Note the reading level of the selection used in any retelling (at, above, or below grade level).

- Note, if possible, if writing pieces and other hands-on projects were completed independently, with peer collaboration, and/or with teacher assistance.

- Be sure the student pays at least one visit to the portfolio each month. At first this should be a guided visit rather than just a quick look-through by the student.

nal is to provide a place to keep track of the process each of you is going through as you try out new portfolio ideas. (This was one of the most valuable tasks that we did. By the end of the year, many teachers had decided that the students should also keep a journal documenting their attempts at the process.) Before you begin each week, review what you wrote the previous week and comment on it. This will force you to take time to reflect on the process and help you to use your experiences to rethink your work. The thoughts and concerns you capture in this journal will provide some of the agenda items and points of discussion for our monthly meetings.

For me, the issue is teaching students to value their own portfolio process and product.

5. Review and Report

At the end of the school year, we will review our work and develop a report of our recommendations. Specifically, we will want to discuss: (a) the advantages/disadvantages of using portfolios, (b) the types of information we were able to collect, (c) how we used the information, (d) how the information compares with information from a standardized test, and (e) suggestions for future work in alternative assessment.

Making Initial Commitments

By February, we had developed a list of learning outcomes and decided that it was time to dive into portfolios headfirst. The following is a summary of portfolio commitments made at specific grade levels. (Note: It's true that these commitments were mostly reading- or writing-related, but these were considered the minimum. We encouraged students to collect materials of all types and curriculum areas in their portfolios.)

Primary

1 retelling (any mode, varied prompts, any text, untimed)
1 teacher-selected piece of writing
1 student-selected contribution (reading or writing)

Intermediate

1 retelling
1 teacher-selected piece of writing with entry slip attached
1 student-selected piece of writing with an entry slip
reading logs
(*It was decided that all papers should have an entry slip attached stating the name of the person entering the work, the date, and why the piece was selected for the portfolio.*)

Middle/Secondary

1 retelling
1 teacher-selected writing

2 student-selected entries with reflection

By this time, we were rapidly moving from seeing the portfolio as a collection of student work to a vehicle for empowering teachers, parents, and students to participate in a of new level of educational responsibility. We grappled with questions such as:

◆ Should portfolios include more than just samples of student work?
◆ To what extent is the portfolio a collaborative venture between teacher and student?
◆ What portion should be self-reflective?
◆ Should a portfolio be used for grading, for conferences, and/or as an aggregation of data?
◆ What value should be placed on the portfolio?
◆ How are portfolios best managed in a classroom?

◆ What are the standards for evaluating portfolio entries as well as the portfolios themselves?

We knew we were moving into a very exciting realm where teachers and students became an assessment team. Rather than having all of the answers, we had a strong feeling that we were moving in a direction that could change our definitions of assessment.

Developing New Contacts

I was very lucky to be able to communicate with other educators from around the country during this process. I saw my role on the committee as a tie between what we were doing in Seattle and what the NEA was doing in its Mastery in Learning Project (MIL). I began writing summaries of our meetings on PsiNet, an NEA-sponsored computer network that linked all of the MIL sites with each other and with some key researchers. In writing about our struggles with "standardizing" portfolios, I received an insightful response from Joe Walters, a researcher for Project Zero at Harvard University *(see box at right)*.

This was a particularly critical time for us to develop new contacts and interject new ideas. When I shared Joe Walters' response with the group, it helped to shift our focus from portfolios as *assessment only* to portfolios and assessment as a part of the larger issue of instruction. We had "lived" with portfolios for several months and realized the following.

◆ Student reflections of their own work were often honest and insightful without the need for teacher comments.

◆ "Muddling through" the process had made us more reflective about the messages we give students and what we are looking for.

◆ While portfolios showed growth, there appeared to be a lack of measurable outcomes.

◆ And, that while teachers were very comfortable with evaluating work on the basis of writing conventions, with portfolios there was a need to look at the work much more holistically.

Moving from Portfolios to Process-Folios

While the original intent of creating portfolios was to obtain the data for a comprehensive assessment/evaluation program that would include equal portions of teacher observation, student artifacts, and tests or testlike data, the portfolios were becoming much more like "process-folios." Because

"It seems to me that there is a trade-off between standardizing portfolios to allow easy comparison of children across school and making portfolios responsive to creative, unique individuals. I tend to prefer the latter when given the choice....

As for standards, I think that standards for portfolios should be created only after portfolio materials have been collected. Rather than starting with the standards, you end with them, building them out of the students' work. Otherwise, we have found, the standards are much too limiting—they tend to be based on specific skills rather than taking the broader perspective.

Standards should encourage connections across subject areas, critical thinking, problem finding, unusual forms of presentation, and so on. This isn't to say that standards are unimportant or that 'anything goes.'

I think with portfolios, you can indeed have it both ways."

—Joe Walters, Researcher for Project Zero
Harvard University

THREE MODELS OF PORTFOLIOS

SHOWCASE
This portfolio merely celebrates work a student has done.

DESCRIPTIVE
This portfolio demonstrates various things a student can do, but provides no evaluation.

EVALUATIVE
Everything in this portfolio is subject to evaluative criteria.

of the student's involvement, portfolios included lots of things that were not necessarily the students' best work. The collected materials showed process, real works in progress, key learning moments, progress over time, failed attempts, special efforts, and, of course, pieces of which the students were especially proud. In selecting pieces from their work folder for a "process-folio," students often selected work that they felt was especially challenging, even though it contained mistakes. In a sense, students themselves were defining the uses and purposes of the portfolio.

One secondary student reflected, "While the mind develops, learns, and experiences, it can relate to previous work. It can compare, draw conclusions. A portfolio contains frozen expressions that we can analyze."

Another student said, "By keeping my portfolio, I learned that not every paper I write is going to be the same. Some will be better and some will be worse than others. By evaluating our papers, I learned what makes some of my papers better than others."

One teacher of elementary students commented, "There is no set time at which all students are expected to accomplish portfolio-related objectives, so there is less chance of perceived failure. Students adopt the philosophy of 'I'll get it.' rather than 'I can't.'"

Changing the Paradigm

By now we realized that to "do portfolios" means to look at instruction and time differently. Again, researcher Joe Walters provided important insight. He told us:

"Portfolios mean an adjustment – teaching and assessing are both happening at the same time and both seen as valuable to learning. Taking the time away from direct instruction in order to give students more time to react to or comment on their work needs to be seen as a productive, instructive use of class time."

One of the most obvious changes was the need to provide class time to actually read and write. The use of a portfolio made the "doing" of reading and writing a priority. It demanded more time than reading and writing instruction.

One of the greatest changes that came about as a result of the use of portfolios and the exploration of alternative assessments was the realization that assessment is integrally tied to teaching strategies; and if our assessments change, so must our teaching. With portfolios as a "shared process," there is no longer the "I teach, you learn." The concepts of learning and instruction can no longer be looked at in isolation from each other. When students become teachers, and teachers model learning, the classroom will truly become a place of "understanding."

Evaluating Portfolios

Toward the end of the year, Sheila Valencia consolidated and summarized some of her findings (based on projects across the country) on portfolios for us. She said there appeared to be three basic models. First, there was the *showcase model* in which students select whatever work they wish to go into the portfolio. A second model, the *descriptive model,* demonstrates various things students can do without evaluating them. In this model, work can be selected by student, teacher, or both. Then there's the *evaluative model* in which every-

thing in the portfolio is subject to evaluative criteria.

Sheila said that from what she had seen, most teachers used a form of showcase. She revealed that when she began working with us, she was hoping we could find a way of making portfolios more evaluative. However, by the end of the year, most of us found that we had portfolios that were descriptive in nature. She added that after working with the group for a year, she's coming to the conclusion that a good portfolio needs to include parts of all three.

I'm not convinced that the evaluation of portfolio contents is even the issue. For me, the issue is teaching students to value their own portfolio process and product, and in so doing, the portfolio becomes a

valuable tool. But, the question as to how you can evaluate the contents of the portfolio continues to resurface. Is the portfolio passed on, sent home, to what purpose?

I suggested to the committee that students revisit their portfolios in June and reflect on the year. The reflection itself could then be passed on to the next teacher, who could then have a picture of what the students, themselves, perceived as their strengths and weaknesses. Being given 30-odd reflections would be a wonderful way of planning course content. Curriculum would be truly student-driven. Many committee members followed this suggestion.

Disbanding the Committee

Before we knew it, our

six-month assignment was up and there were no funds earmarked for its continuance in the fall. We left that June not knowing if we would ever meet as a group again. The co-chairs, Elaine Aoki, Robert Vaughan, and Sheila Valencia were as concerned as we were about the "death" of the committee. Sharing our victories, insights, and frustrations had made us a strongly knit group. We knew we had not accomplished everything we had set out to do (especially when it came to determining how to evaluate portfolios), but few of us would argue the fact that we had learned some very important things about the process of teaching and learning.

We had learned some things about ourselves, too. The lines between administration and teaching corps blurred when time was given to thoughtfully exploring issues crucial to children and their educational progress.

As a group we departed, just as committed to finding "new" and effective ways to assess children as before, just as committed to continuing our exploration of portfolios and sharing our findings with others. We left our group work unfinished, but even two years after we ceased to exist as a committee, we are still in communication with each other, and still eager to share our latest experiences with each other. Elaine continues to try to get funding for our group to continue. The district now has an "Assessment Swap-Meet" once a month and many

members of the committee have contributed.

Carol Lake and Chris Morningstar, fellow Kimball teachers and members of our school Alternative Assessment Committee, are working with me to compile "A Look at Alternative Assessment" report for the other 30 Seattle Schools in our Schools for the 21st Century project. Rather than receive compensation, we have asked for resources to get all Kimball teachers on board for portfolios by 1993-94. One suggestion that came out of the committee was that teachers should work as teams to provide on-going support and dialogue about the process. Because Kimball is an open space, team-teaching school, this will be important, yet relatively easy for colleagues to implement. We also feel

the need to continue to share our discoveries as well as questions and problems over PsiNet with the NEA/National Center for Innovation schools.

Looking Back

Our initial interest group of teachers could have remained just as it began, by meeting after school and posing questions and challenges we faced on an informal basis, but somewhere along the line we asked the right questions and sought the "good" solutions and were noticed. In a district the size of Seattle, this is rare indeed. In a district where adversarial relationships between administrators and teachers were more often than not "the name of the game," we found critical friends who cared about what we cared

about. We found creative ways of getting help from the local university. And, most important, we found each other.

Since the beginnings of this assessment group, others of us have continued to see that we can change things. Call it restructuring. Call it taking risks. We, as teachers, have stuck our necks out to change what we felt needed changing.

In the past, our local teachers' association and school district have often picked members for various committees. Now many of us volunteer to serve on those committees and recommend others we know who have a relevant interest or level of expertise. We feel confident that if we have research on our side and know what is best for kids, that we can change things. ◆

Reader Reflections

Insights: _____

_____

_____

_____

_____

_____

Actions for Our School (District) to Consider: _____

_____

_____

_____

_____

_____

_____

_____

_____

The Manhattan Assessment Project

2

"Individuals and small groups of teachers and principals must create the school and professional culture they want."

Fullan, Hargreaves 1991

Manhattan, Kansas, known as the "Little Apple," is full of "big ideas." It is a small yet innovative district that is known to get a whole lot of results out of the limited financial resources available to a typical rural community.

Our school, Amanda Arnold Elementary, is one of nine K-6 schools that serves this rural community. In an eight-year-old building filled to capacity, we continue to use all the resources we can muster to work toward our vision of developing every child to his or her potential.

For several years, the Kansas National Education Association awarded us grants for staff development. Thanks to this support as well as to important partnerships with educators at Kansas State University and to participation in the National Education Association/IBM School Renewal Network, our staff was able to develop a process approach to teaching in math, science, and the language arts.

We three teachers (two of us teach first grade, the other teaches fourth) were proud of our school's progress, yet we felt the standard assessment yardsticks we were using failed to truly measure how individual students were learning in a process approach. We sat down and discussed the strengths and weaknesses of our current practices and decided that we could better align

LISA BIETAU, Fourth Grade Teacher
BARBARA MAUGHMER, First Grade Teacher
JOYCE CRILL, First Grade Teacher
Amanda Arnold Elementary School
Manhattan, Kansas

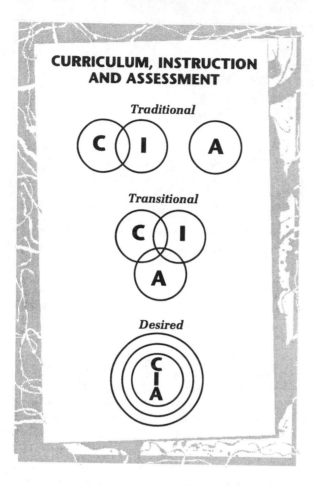

CURRICULUM, INSTRUCTION AND ASSESSMENT

Traditional

C I A

Transitional

C I
A

Desired

C
I
A

our behaviors to our beliefs if we adjusted our assessment practices.

We decided to turn this idea into an action-research project. Our official objective became: *"to create alternative assessment strategies that collect data and focus on important student outcomes in three curricularly integrated classrooms."*

We applied for and received a $750 innovation mini-grant from our school district to work on this project. The small grant helped us purchase supplies for the project, but more importantly, it stood for permission to venture down a new path with district endorsement.

Outlining the Research Project

We not only wanted the district's endorsement, we wanted support and participation from our 75 students and their parents. We turned to the NEA/IBM School Renewal Network for advice on the matter.

Among other things, the School Renewal Network links teachers to researchers and other teachers through an electronic network called PsiNet. After considerable interchange with PsiNet participants, we developed the following goals that we hoped would: (1) integrate assessment and learning, and (2) actively engage students and their parents in the process.

◆ Seek a better match between students and teaching and assessment practices.

◆ Use a variety of assessment processes.

◆ Build a strong partnership between parent(s), student, and teacher by giving each member of the team a role in assessment and goal setting.

◆ Establish curricular outcomes that are essential to the success of all students.

◆ Establish at least two individual goals for each child during an early fall conference between parent(s), teacher, and child.

◆ Use this action-research project to model peer coaching, action research, and risk-taking for staff and students.

◆ Empower parents, teachers, and students to collectively challenge traditions and practices of the school and replace them with practices that enhance achievement for all students.

◆ Use the School Renewal Network to its fullest — learn from it as well as contribute site-specific knowledge to it.

Summer Preparations

We spent the summer reviewing current education literature and communicating with practitioners who were considering the same questions. By the end of those three months, we had done the following.

◆ Compiled a collection of research on alternative assessment and selected pieces to share with parents in the fall

◆ Devised checklists of grade-level outcomes in all subject areas (copies of state and district outcomes and current curriculum guides helped us create these)

◆ Decided to use checklists of outcomes, student portfolios, and student goal-setting as alternative assessment tools

◆ Set time lines for the project, allowing us to keep on track and communicate the big picture to parents (see Portfolio Reproducible 2.1)

Parent Involvement

Every year, Amanda Arnold conducts a Back-to-School Night just before school starts where students and parents can meet the teachers. That fall at Back-to-School Night, we not only introduced ourselves but gave attendees a brief description of our assessment project and a short journal article on alternative assessment.

We also informally surveyed parents and students on their perceptions of school and grades. Overall, they didn't have strong feelings against letter grades, probably because our neighborhood is made up of parents and children who for the most part have been successful in a standard educational system.

Two weeks later, prepared with background on these perceptions as well as with an official rationale, more research handouts, and a detailed plan for change (Portfolio Reproducible 2.1), we conducted a one-hour parent orientation session. We handed out our materials and discussed our assessment plans in detail. There would be no grades, we told parents. Personal goal sheets, checklists of outcomes, and narrative reports would take their place. Although the parents felt no urgency to change, they said they understood the research that supported our desire to change and that they were willing to see us try our new ideas.

We assured them we would conference at the end of every quarter to

guarantee good communication. We also said we would send home weekly classroom newsletters that would chronicle our progress.

We decided we could better align our behaviors with our beliefs if we adjusted our assessment practices.

At the end of the session, we then asked parents to sign up for an evening in October in which they along with their child would meet with the teacher to set two personal goals for the year.

PORTFOLIOS LINK . . .

◆ Curriculum, instruction, and assessment

◆ Student responsibility, teaching, and learning

◆ Grade level, unit, and lesson outcomes with district outcomes

◆ School and community

◆ Teachers, students, and parents

Setting Personal Goals

We spent a lot of time during October conducting the goal-setting meetings. The first grade teachers visited students' homes for these meetings; the fourth grade teacher, who taught a larger group of students, opted for school visits after school hours.

During the meetings, each parent-teacher-child team agreed upon two major goals for the school year as well as specific activities that would help determine whether the student met these goals. All agreements were written on an official goal sheet like the one in Portfolio Reproducible 2.2.

First grade goals were rather general, usually academic or social in nature. Fourth grade goals were set in areas of specific need and/or challenge.

Parent(s), teacher, and child all understood that these goals would be regularly assessed and revised throughout the year.

Refining Assessment Strategies

We began using a variety of assessment strategies in our classrooms. These included observation, performance/demonstration with established criteria, and checklists of various skills.

We instructed students to store the written results of these assessments, along with work we selected together at the end of a thematic unit or project, in portfolios. We also encouraged students to select work on their own that they felt demonstrated something important. We told them the portfolio selections didn't have to be in written form. They could include audiotape recordings of readings or reports, videotapes of demonstrations, computer disks of various work, photographs, artwork, and so on.

Portfolio structures and management varied from teacher to teacher. For the portfolios themselves, the two primary classrooms used giant envelopes made of tagboard, while the fourth grade stored its work in magazine file boxes, folders, and three-ring notebooks.

Teachers chose various ways to regularly review these portfolios with students and to have students reflect on evidence of growth. Often students reflected in writing. They would answer such questions as:

◆ What does this sample of work show that you can do? Write sentences that explain. (i.e., Think about what you did and what you learned. What criteria on your outcomes checklists did you meet?)

◆ Write sentences that tell what you did well in this exercise.

◆ Write about any future goals this activity has

lead you to set.

Many times, fourth-grade study buddies were asked to help first graders write personal reflections.

Parent-Teacher-Student Conferences

In addition to the goal-setting conferences at the beginning of the year, we conducted parent-teacher-student conferences at the end of every nine-week quarter. Students led the conferences by discussing their portfolios and goals with their parents and the teacher.

The teacher would then pull out a set of outcomes checklists (also called a learning profile). Next to each outcome, the teacher would give the child a rating that indicated how he or she was progressing toward the outcome (see Portfolio Reproducible 2.3). For example, on the fourth grade profile, 1 = not yet demonstrated; 3 = in progress; and 5 = consistently demonstrated.

We followed up every conference with a written narrative that summarized the agreements made in the conference discussion. After everyone read the narrative, it was stored in the child's portfolio along with the child's current goal-setting sheet and learning profile.

At the last three-way conference, parent(s), teacher, and student made a final assessment on student progress and goal achievement and set some goals for the summer. The three-way team then selected a few pieces of work from the child's portfolio for next year's teacher to use. Parents took the remaining portfolio materials home.

Looking Back

Did the Manhattan Assessment Project accomplish what it set out to do? Did it create better strategies for measuring student outcomes? We think so. Sure, we had to deal with our share of time-management challenges and uncertainties. (Some parents continued to ask: "Where is my child in relation to ...?") But it was worth it.

As the year proceeded, students began to articulate learning goals and criteria, something our previous students had never done. As a result, learning was more reflective, active, and memorable.

Mistakes became

POSSIBILITIES FOR PORTFOLIO ENTRIES

1. Learning-Log Entries
2. Writing Samples
3. Spelling Samples
4. Handwriting Samples
5. Various Text Pages that Students Have Mastered
6. Audiotape Recordings of Readings, Reports, or Demonstrations
7. Videotape Recordings of Readings, Reports, or Demonstrations
8. Computer Disks of Various Work
9. Artwork
11. Photographs
12. Lists of Books Read
13. Skills Checklists
14. Self-Assessment Sheets
15. Personal Goals Sheets
16. Outcomes Checklists
17. Assessment Narratives (Agreements made during conferences)
18. Parent Reflections on Portfolio

"learning opportunities" as the students watched us successfully model the same types of risk-taking and "tolerance for change" we asked of them. All of this empowered the children to be a part of our assessment investigation. They were able to experience the thrill of problem solving in the real world. They reflected with their teachers and parents as we together tried to invent new ways to accomplish our goals. In short, parents, teachers, and students became a learning community.

As professionals, we three teachers felt that we made a difference by contributing to the pool of ideas currently being tested in the redesigning of assessment. We were active participants who had acquired expertise to offer others traveling down the road that tests the barriers and boundaries of the status quo.

The Project Today

The Manhattan Assessment Project is now a growing cadre of local teachers in pursuit of assessment alternatives. The teachers have copied some parts of the original project, adapted other parts, and created some of their own parts. These days, our district conducts regular study groups on assessment at which many of these teachers participate. Amanda Arnold even has its own small study group that meets weekly to discuss ideas and issues related to assessment.

During the past year, our original team of three has revised its learning profiles and rewritten its time lines. We are still struggling with the need for developing appropriate grade-level standards to communicate to parents. One of us feels this should be explained by showing individual growth of the student on a continuum and not in relationship to a grade-level standard. Another of us feels parents have a right to know how their child rates in relationship to the rest of the class. And another would like to see standard examples set for curriculum outcomes (i.e., show parents a typical piece of first grade writing, reading text, and so on).

In summary, we continue to log milestones and accumulate evidence in the areas of portfolios and other forms of alternative assessment. We find comfort in our capacity to sustain this continual journey, because we have learned, as researcher John Schaar so eloquently says:

"The future is not some place we are going to, but one we are creating. The paths are not to be found, but made, and the activity of making them changes both the maker and the destination."◆

PROPOSED TIME LINE FOR 1991-92 ASSESSMENT PROJECT

September	October	November	December
◆ Collect parent and student views on current reporting system. ◆ Provide overview of assessment project at Back-to-School-Night Presentation. ◆ Provide more specific info at one-hour Parent Orientation Session. ◆ Set conference dates for personal student goal-setting.	◆ Conduct parent-teacher-student meeting to set personal student goals for the year. ◆ Have students begin to select portfolio work and to include self-reflections of this work.	◆ Conduct first series of parent-teacher-student conferences and provide follow-up narratives.	◆ Have students continue portfolio selection and self-reflection.

January	February•March•April	May
◆ Conduct second series of parent-teacher-student conferences and provide follow-up narratives. ◆ Update outcomes form. ◆ Review personal student goals.	◆ Have students continue portfolio selection and self-reflection. ◆ Continue to assess students according to prescribed outcomes. ◆ Help students pursue their personal goals.	◆ Have students complete portfolios. ◆ Conduct final parent-teacher-student conferences: assess achievement of personal goals, share portfolio, and set summer goals. ◆ Post-assess the project.

Personal Goals Sheet - (Completed Sample)

Student: Sue B. **Grade:** 4 **Teacher:** Bietau

Goal

To increase revision strategies in daily writing

Objective

Quarter

1. To improve use of homonyms

2. To keep record of spelling errors and use as part of weekly list

3. To read all writing carefully and revise before handing in

Assessment Activity

1. A) Make a homonym reference sheet.
   B) Create a homonym game.

2 A) Underline "guessed" words; write errors in spelling folder; use for personal word lists.

3. A) Make a star ☆ by a name indicating student revision has been completed.

Goal

To continue to develop leadership skills

Objective

Quarter

1. To develop time management strategies

2. To organize and lead the "Scrapbook Club"

3. To represent class in S.A.C.

4. To co-lead the "Environmental Club"

Assessment Activity

1. A) Use calendar.
   B) Use Homework Tracker.

2. A) Do a Captain's Report. B) Do a scrapbook evaluation.

3. A) Make weekly reports and keep a folder.
   B) Make weekly presentations to class.

4. A) Do a Captain's Report. B) Do project evaluations.

LEARNING PROFILE

Student: _____ Grade: _____ Teacher: _____

KEY:

◩	**Not Assessed**	
1	**Not Yet Demonstrated**	
3	**In Progress**	
5	**Consistently Demonstrated Mastery**	

	I	II	III	IV

I. Contributes to a Learning Community

A. Eagerly accepts a challenge.

B. Uses worktime productively.

C. Demonstrates self-control.

D. Expresses enjoyment after achievement.

E. Cooperates with others.

F. Contributes to group work.

G. Considers a variety of alternatives when solving problems.

H. Makes responsible choices independently.

I. Considers other points of view.

J. Plans, organizes, and carries through a task to completion.

K. Demonstrates organizational skills:

  1. Takes responsibility for completing homework.

  2. Takes responsibility for completing the assignments in school.

  3. Maintains an organized work area.

  4. Respects the rights and properties of others.

II. Investigates Our Global Community

A. Locates place on Earth:

  1. Understands physical vs. political boundaries.

  2. Locates continents and oceans.

  3. Uses latitude and longitude to find locations.

B. Explores Earth's regions:

  1. Investigates regions of Kansas.

  2. Identifies regions of the United States.

  3. Explores regions of Africa.

  4. Explores diverse regions of the world.

I · II · III · IV

☐ ☐ ☐ ☐
☐ ☐ ☐ ☐
☐ ☐ ☐ ☐
☐ ☐ ☐ ☐

C. Develops an understanding of world cultures:

1. Compares individuals in a learning community. ☐☐☐☐

2. Investigates Native Americans of the plains past/present. ☐☐☐☐

3. Demonstrates an understanding of an African culture. ☐☐☐☐

4. Demonstrates an understanding of world cultures. ☐☐☐☐

D. Investigates human efforts in the environment:

1. Identifies patterns of human use of Earth's resources. ☐☐☐☐

2. Investigates people's' inventiveness to adapt to different environments. These include:

   a. Patterns of change, ☐☐☐☐☐

   b. Models and simulations at work, ☐☐☐☐☐

   c. Diversity and unity in our world, ☐☐☐☐☐

   d. Interacting systems of our world. ☐☐☐☐☐

3. Investigates people's effect on the balance of nature. ☐☐☐☐☐

III. Communication and Investigation Within a Learning Community

A. Applies reading skills:

1. Demonstrates a positive attitude toward reading. ☐☐☐☐☐

2. Understands what is read. ☐☐☐☐☐

3. Summarizes important information. ☐☐☐☐☐

4. Makes connections to his/her background. ☐☐☐☐☐

5. Uses strategies to decode new words. ☐☐☐☐☐

B. Locates and uses reference materials for researching information. ☐☐☐☐

C. Demonstrates ability to communicate in writing. ☐☐☐☐

1. Demonstrates an understanding of the writing process. ☐☐☐☐

2. Demonstrates ability to write for different purposes:

   a. Report writing, ☐☐☐☐☐

   b. Narrative writing, ☐☐☐☐☐

   c. Creative writing, ☐☐☐☐☐

   d. Letter writing, ☐☐☐☐☐

   e. Descriptive writing. ☐☐☐☐☐

I   II   III   IV

3. Demonstrates application of the following writing traits:

   a. Idea/content,

   b. Organization,

   c. Voice/tone,

   d. Effective word choice,

   e. Sentence fluency,

   f. Writing conventions.

     (1) Uses complete sentences and punctuation.

     (2) Revises spelling errors.

     (3) Masters weekly spelling patterns.

4. Organizes written communications:

   a. Forms letters and numbers legibly.

   b. Organizes work on the page.

D. Listens and shares in a learning community:

   1. Asks questions.

   2. Participates in discussions.

   3. Follows a sequence of directions.

IV. Applying Problem-Solving and Investigative Strategies

A. Understands and recalls basic facts in:

   1. Addition,

   2. Subtraction,

   3. Multiplication,

   4. Division.

B. Applies problem-solving strategies:

   1. Estimates and checks.

   2. Draws it out.

   3. Makes tables and graphs.

   4. Looks for patterns.

   5. Acts it out.

C. Geometry —Develops spatial thinking:

   1. Understands geometric terms.

   2. Identifies geometric patterns, properties, and relation-

I   II   III   IV

☐ ☐ ☐ ☐   ☐ ☐ ☐ ☐   ☐ ☐ ☐ ☐ ☐

☐ ☐ ☐ ☐   ☐ ☐ ☐ ☐   ☐ ☐ ☐ ☐ ☐

☐ ☐ ☐ ☐   ☐ ☐ ☐ ☐   ☐ ☐ ☐ ☐ ☐

☐ ☐ ☐ ☐   ☐ ☐ ☐ ☐   ☐ ☐ ☐ ☐ ☐

ships.

D. Makes mathematical connections to the real world:

1. Formulates the problem.

2. Collects data.

3. Analyzes results.

E. Communicates ideas to others:

1. Describes solutions in writing.

2. Explains solutions in writing.

3. Uses math vocabulary to explain solutions.

F. Makes accurate/detailed observations.

G. Accurately measures:

1. Uses appropriate measurement unit.

2. Uses reasonable estimates of measurement.

H. Applies classification strategies.

I. Formulates predictions.

J. Uses technology to assist learning.

Insights: _____

_____

_____

_____

_____

_____

Actions for Our School (District) to Consider: _____

_____

_____

_____

_____

_____

_____

_____

_____

SCHOOLWIDE *Portfolios*

3

I am a mathematics teacher at Metro High School in Cedar Rapids, Iowa. I have also been a member of the building committee that has been working on implementing portfolios and alternative assessment since we began the process in the spring of 1990. At Metro we have defined portfolios as,

"a record of learning that focuses on the student's work and her/his reflections on that work.

Material is collected through a collaborative effort between the student and staff members and is indicative of progress toward our school's prescribed essential outcomes."

While portfolios in some schools focus on literacy or writing across the curriculum, ours is more inclusive. It includes all curriculum areas and all modes of learning from writing samples to audiocassettes to hands-on projects.

Even though I have been asked to write this piece about our efforts, I want to stress that the progress we have made, and are continuing to make, is the result of the hard work and dedication of a number of individuals at Metro.

I have decided to begin with a brief explanation of our school to provide a context in which to view subsequent remarks. This will be followed by my thoughts on how we arrived at the decision to implement portfolios, a chronology of our past efforts, future plans, and personal reflections on the entire process.

DONALD DAWS

Mathematics Teacher
Metro High School
Cedar Rapids, Iowa

Setting

Metro is the alternative high school for the Cedar Rapids Community School District. Our

ADVICE FOR NEW PORTFOLIO IMPLEMENTERS

• Take into account that the change process will raise personal as well as educational concerns. These personal concerns will need to be addressed before progress can be made on the educational considerations.

• Remember that the implementation of portfolios is a slow and evolving process.

students come from all areas of the city as well as from the surrounding metropolitan and rural areas. We serve approximately 600 students who range in age from 14 through 21. Our students are about equally divided between males and females. About 450 of our students are enrolled in our morning or afternoon programs and are working toward earning a high school diploma. The remaining students, about 150, are either enrolled in our Learning Center where they are studying for their General Equivalency Diploma, or are temporarily inactive due to placement in rehabilitation or correctional facilities.

Our curriculum is designed to allow students to meet the prescribed graduation requirements of the district, although we often meet these requirements by using less traditional methods. We have no band, chorus, or traditional extracurricular activities. However, our students may participate in these activities at one of the district's conventional high schools. Physical education requirements are met through the completion of individual "contracts" between the student and his or her advisor.

We have 37 teachers on the Metro faculty. Most of us serve as advisors for 10 to 25 students. Our role as an advisor is to help a student be successful at Metro. This includes assisting with educational planning; developing behavior-management strategies if necessary; and serving as a liaison between the school and parents/guardians, social workers, probation officers, and others when appropriate. One of our goals is to visit each advisee's home at least once a trimester and meet with our advisee and his or her parent(s)/guardian(s), to answer questions and to discuss school progress. In addition to these one-to-one conferences, we meet periodically in advisor/advisee groups to complete physical education contracts, pre-register for classes, set academic and attendance goals as well as other activities.

Teachers generally meet with students for six periods of an eight-period day, Monday through Thursday. For example, my current teaching assignment includes three individualized Algebra/Geometry classes and one two-period team-taught Math/ Science Projects course. My sixth period is scheduled for coordinating two projects — Metro's involvement with the NEA National Center for Innovation's School Renewal Network and our new IBM Remedial Skills Lab. Our administration makes an effort to limit class sizes to between 15 and 20 students for classes taught by one teacher and between 20 and 30 students for team-taught classes.

Our students do not attend classes on Friday. We generally begin that day with a meeting of the entire faculty to discuss concerns and to coordinate Metro's program. During the rest of the day, we either meet in a variety of committees and/or make home visits to our advisees.

Basis for the Implementation Of Portfolios

Metro has been a member of Ted Sizer's Coalition of Essential Schools since 1985 and a part of the NEA's School Renewal Network since 1989. Our connection

with these organizations, the involvement of several of our faculty in graduate programs, and a continual growth in the percentage of our students enrolling in post-secondary institutions, led to a number of us expressing a need to raise the academic expectations for our students. Further, we felt that if we increased our expectations we also needed to develop new methods to document the student's progress in ways that expanded on our written narrative evaluations. Enter portfolios – a vehicle that would allow us to document authentic work in a central location and then use it as a tool in education planning and program evaluation.

Chronology
Spring 1990

Each spring, schools in

our district are required to develop a School Improvement Plan. This consists of a set of goals and subsequent strategies that the school staff plans to concentrate on the following year. To address our concerns with student expectations and additional documentation, the Metro staff determined that one of our committees for the implementation of the 1990/91 School Improvement Plan would focus on issues of curriculum, instruction, and assessment. This committee of about 10 to 12 teachers, has remained in place for the last three years. About half of us have served on the committee for the entire time. The remaining members have varied from year to year due to changing interests and

the inclusion of newly hired faculty members.

1990/91 School Year

Our committee decided, almost from our initial meeting in the fall, that portfolios and alternative assessments were two areas we would study and eventually recommend for adoption by the entire Metro staff. During the 1990/91 school year, our work in

Portfolio implementation is a slow and evolving process.

these areas focused primarily on developing a theoretical understanding of, and research basis for, our beliefs. Our group gathered, studied, and discussed numerous journal articles, research papers, and materials from the School Renewal Network that related to portfolios and alternative assessment. We found the work of Ted Sizer and the Coalition of Essential Schools as well as that of Joe Walters, William Spady, Grant Wiggins, and Dennie Palmer Wolf (see Selected References section of this book) to be particularly helpful. Several of us also attended a state-level conference on restructuring and reported our findings to the other committee members. Finally, the district's Director of Research and Evaluation made a presentation to interested faculty members on the use of alternative assessments.

In the spring of 1991, we began a pilot program on portfolios. Several teachers labeled folders with student names and began collecting material from their classes for the portfolios. We also began talking individually with other faculty members to explain the portfolio concept and to encourage them to submit student work.

1991/92 School Year

In the fall of 1991, we decided it was time to present our committee's findings to the entire faculty. In October our group led a discussion to explain where it was in the process and to gather additional ideas and concerns regarding portfolios.

Following this discussion, our committee developed a two-page handout that included our definition of portfolios, a rationale for their use, a proposed outline for mechanical procedures, and a description of the relationship between material selection and the proposed essential outcomes (see Portfolio Reproducibles 3.1 and 3.2).

In mid-November we presented this handout, a draft of a portfolio response-sheet to be completed by both the teacher and student, and several pertinent articles at a Friday meeting. Time was made available to read the articles and to study the handout and response sheet. This was followed by a discussion to acquire additional input on our proposals.

In addition to these formal strategies, we continued to talk with teachers on an informal basis. We felt this was necessary to alleviate individual concerns, answer questions regarding our rationale, and to encourage participation.

During the latter part of the year there seemed to be an unspoken shift in our philosophy: our committee focused its energies on increasing the level of teachers' submission of material and de-emphasized the need to connect these projects to one or more of the essential outcomes. The connection to essential outcomes had not been eliminated, but rather deferred in order to make the use of portfolios less cumbersome and/or threatening to beginners.

1992/93 School Year

In fall 1992 our committee continued to work

informally to explain the process, and rationale for, portfolios. At this point, we began to see some benefits from our efforts. Staff participation increased and some of our students began to view their work in class in terms of inclusion in their portfolios. Some students were even asking their advisors for an opportunity to inspect their portfolios. Mary Vasey, our committee chairperson, decided to incorporate a portfolio review in the Preparing to Graduate Course for last-term seniors.

Our committee also modified our portfolio response-sheet (see Portfolio Reproducible 3.3). We did this in an effort to simplify the process for both students and teachers and to encourage a greater degree of reflection. We also suggested that teachers include a portfolio review as part of an advisor/advisee group meeting.

Current Work
In a parallel project, our committee is now working with teachers within departments to study how their departmental goals and objectives mesh with the essential outcomes. We plan to also develop examples of demonstrations or projects that will assess these outcomes.

Future Directions
We have made, and are continuing to make, progress in our move toward portfolios and alternative assessment, but there are several unfinished areas. Our committee is still trying to help a few faculty members understand the process and rationale for portfolios. They still either do not accept that change is necessary, fear the effects portfolios will have on their teaching methods, or view the portfolio process as additional work. We continue to encourage and assist them in developing project-oriented curricula and in integrating reflection into their classes in lieu of current instructional practices. Our committee also plans to continue to refine the portfolio response-sheet to further assist teachers and students in the assessment and reflection process. We intend to work with our administration to develop methods to support the use of portfolios. Advisors must have time to work with advisees on a one-to-one basis to discuss their portfolios and to use them for educational planning. Finally, we will need to eventually integrate portfolios with our essential outcomes as part of our overall assessment program.

In short, at this point in time, we have portfolios, but we are still

MORE ADVICE FOR NEW PORTFOLIO IMPLEMENTERS

• Begin the process by having a small group of committed people read and study the literature pertaining to portfolios. This group can then synthesize the information and make a presentation of its findings to the entire faculty.

• Develop both formal and informal methods to keep the faculty informed of developments, to answer questions, and to alleviate concerns.

• Be aware that starting an innovation like portfolios may bring into question other school practices, such as instructional methods and the departmentalization of the curriculum.

working on developing methods to use portfolios as a means of assessment – assessment of both our students' progress and needs of our curriculum and instruction.

Reflections

As I reflect on the last three years of portfolio implementation at Metro, five crucial areas surface. These are the time frame

Much of the research on change suggests that it takes from five to seven years for substantive change to occur.

for implementation, the development of a theoretical basis, implementation methods, attention to personal concerns, and curricular changes.

Time Frame for Implementation

As Barb Coates, one of our committee members, noted: "Portfolio implementation is a slow and evolutionary process."

After almost three years, there are still a few teachers who either don't understand or don't accept a system of portfolios and alternative assessment. We are refining, and will continue to refine, our portfolio response-sheets. We are continuing to develop methods that will allow for the effective and efficient use of portfolios by teachers, students, and advisors. Finally, and most importantly, we have not yet integrated portfolios and our es-

sential outcomes in a cohesive manner.

I think when we started considering portfolios we felt that we would have full implementation within a few years. Some of us have become somewhat discouraged with the slow rate of change. However, we should not have been surprised. Much of the research on the change process suggests that it takes from five to 10 years for substantive change to occur.

Development of a Theoretical Basis

I believe the process we used to develop our rationale for portfolios and alternative assessment was relatively solid. We started with a small group of individuals that was committed to the use of portfolios and

willing to spend extra time researching the issue. Our group read and discussed a wide range of theoretical and practical material and then synthesized the information for discussion by the entire Metro faculty.

I also believe it was beneficial to distribute several key articles to all teachers and to provide time at a staff meeting for reading and discussing the material. Giving our faculty time to think about our proposals, ask questions, receive additional information, and then rethink the ideas, seemed to increase acceptance and alleviate concerns about portfolios.

Our use of both formal and informal methods proved useful. Our committee explained the key concepts and issues in a large group setting. This seemed to begin the development of a common set of understandings. The informal, individual discussions between our committee members and other teachers built on these understandings and served to ease some of the personal concerns.

Implementation Methods

An idea we found useful, although it took us almost a year to move in this direction, was to separate the issues of portfolios and alternative assessment. Implementing both concepts as a unified package seemed to be more than some of our teachers could manage. As a result we seemed to be making little progress. When we concentrated on increasing participa-

tion and de-emphasized the need to relate the projects to the essential outcomes, teacher acceptance of portfolios seemed to increase. I don't believe this was due to a lack of harmony with the outcomes, rather, some people seemed to need an opportunity to develop and incorporate routines involved in the portfolio process before they felt able to address and coordinate portfolio use with the outcomes. In fact, having a portfolio process in place has made it easier for us to begin focusing on the essential outcomes. However, we still need to address the extremely difficult process of linking these two areas.

This method is an example of what researcher Michael Fullan refers to

as Ready-Fire-Aim. We developed a rationale for portfolios (got ready), focused on increasing teacher participation (fired), and now we need to connect portfolios and the essential outcomes (aim).

Attention to Personal Concerns

During our initial discussions with the faculty, personal concerns were much more an issue than educational considerations. These concerns fell into two broad areas. The first related to both mechanical and procedural issues. Teachers asked questions like: "What will the portfolios look like?"; "Where will they be stored?"; "Who will be responsible for selecting, filing, and sorting student work?" These

seemed much more urgent than ones like: "How will students benefit from portfolios?"

After a lengthy discussion, we arrived at tentative solutions to these questions. The folders would be stored in file cabinets located in an office near the library. One of our secretaries volunteered to label new folders and file student work. We decided that the teacher and student within a class would determine which materials would be included in the portfolios, and the advisor and advisee would be responsible for using the portfolio in educational planning.

The second, and related issue, dealt with time. Several of our teachers raised concerns regarding building in time for teachers and students to complete response sheets and providing advisors with the time to meet with advisees and work with them on a one-to-one basis.

Although our committee was not prepared for this reaction, we could have anticipated these concerns.

The literature on the change process stresses the personal nature of change. Until the personal concerns of the individuals affected by the change are addressed, little progress can be made on the educational issues.

Curricular Changes

Probably the most profound effect on me personally has been the realization that portfolios, and their use in assessment, necessitates a change in the way I teach mathematics. If I truly believe in the process, then I can no longer have students move in a lock-step fashion through the textbook.

The other math teachers and I now intend to develop a set of key concepts in each area of mathematics. These will be used to develop projects that address the essential outcomes, either for use in our classes or in conjunction with teachers from other subject areas in interdisciplinary courses. Completed projects will be included in each student's portfolio for use by the student and his or her advisor. We will also use these projects to continually assess and update our mathematics program at Metro.

Conclusion

At Metro we have made, and are continuing to make, progress regarding the efficient and effective use of portfolios. Up to this point, our committee has done very well in some areas and not quite as well in others. I believe we could have foreseen and alleviated some of the difficulties we encountered if we had been more attuned to the literature on the change process. My suggestion to people about to begin portfolio implementation, or any innovation, would be to read, study, and incorporate the practical and theoretical findings of this body of knowledge as they start out on their journey. ◆

Definition

A *portfolio* is a record of learning that focuses on the student's work and her/his reflection on that work. Material is collected through a collaborative effort between the student and staff members and is indicative of progress toward the essential outcomes.

Rationale

Portfolios can provide a vehicle to:

1. assist students and staff members in assessing their progress toward acquiring the essential outcomes;

2. determine personal strengths, weaknesses, and preferences;

3. document the extent of students' willingness to take risks;

4. increase student self-esteem;

5. practice and emphasize reflection;

6. emphasize the importance of both product and process;

7. develop material for a senior seminar/exhibition that might serve as a portfolio for college and/or work;

8. assist with end-of-term evaluations;

9. develop both short- and long-term goals; and

10. provide staff members with information to adjust course content and offerings to meet student needs.

Mechanics

Location

- Material will be stored in file boxes until and unless a more suitable method emerges.
- File boxes will be stored in Room 207.

Acquisition of Materials

The committee recommends that at least once per term the student and teacher select material for inclusion in the portfolio. The most appropriate time for this discussion and the completion of a reflection sheet, is immediately following the completion of the project. Bonnie D. has agreed to file the material in student folders.

The committee recommends that at least once per term the student and advisor meet to review the portfolio. This conference can be used to develop the student's schedule for the next term and to establish goals in specific areas. Further, it can provide a method to highlight areas of growth and/or strength and emphasize the multidisciplinary aspects of central ideas.

Essential Outcomes and the Selection of Material

Following a review of prior staff discussions and a sampling of the literature, the Curriculum/Student Outcomes Committee developed four preliminary essential outcomes.

Students, upon graduation from Metro High School will be:

- **Information Literate** – Able to gather, organize, evaluate, synthesize, and communicate information.
- **Self-Directed and Future-Oriented** – Able to set goals, to be aware of a wide range of possibilities and their consequences, and to meet and re-evaluate goals.
- **Community Contributors** – Able to collaborate, participate, empathize, and communicate.
- **Innovative/Creative Producers**

It is recommended that material selected for inclusion in the portfolio relate to at least one of the four essential outcomes.

METRO HIGH SCHOOL PORTFOLIO RESPONSE SHEET

Name: _____ Advisor: _____ Date: _____

Class: _____ Teacher: _____

Please describe your project. What did you do? Please be specific. _____

_____

_____

Where did you get your ideas?
(Did you read about them? Ask someone? Use your own imagination?)

_____

_____

What did you like most about doing this project? _____

_____

_____

What frustrated you most? _____

_____

_____

What do you wish you had done differently? _____

_____

Teacher comments: _____

_____

Did You . . .

write	compare
organize	classify
observe	analyze
investigate	contrast
question	specify
explain	interview
perceive	video
understand	survey
describe	experiment
envision	invent
edit	draw
construct	photograph
relate	present
put in your	share
own words	express
identify	create
solve	list
outline	choreograph
plan	report
eliminate	respond
forecast	learn
summarize	brainstorm
shape	support
generalize	draft
think	sketch
demonstrate	finish...?
practice	

Reader Reflections

Insights: _____

_____

_____

_____

_____

Actions for Our School (District) to Consider: _____

_____

_____

_____

_____

_____

_____

*Probably the most profound effect on me personally
has been the realization that portfolios,
and their use in assessment,
necessitates a change in the way I teach mathematics.*

LITERACY PORTFOLIOS
In the Early Childhood Classroom

4

Recently, at the forty-eighth Annual Conference of the Association for Supervision and Curriculum Development, I and two other educators from South Brunswick Township, New Jersey, organized a presentation on "Using Portfolios to Improve Instruction and Increase Accountability."

We were expecting approximately 40 participants at our session. Instead, we were greeted by at least 150 very eager and excited educators, anxiously huddled outside the door to a very small presentation room.

As soon as group members learned we were the presenters, one by one they approached us and asked for special consideration for admission to an obviously overbooked session.

"I've been standing here for one hour," said a woman in desperation, "You have to let me in!"

The group pleaded, "Please see if you can get a larger room. We need to learn about your portfolios."

Others were begging for "at least handouts" so they had some type of information to take away with them.

CHERYL POLAKOWSKI

Full-Day Kindergarten Teacher
Constable School
Kendall Park, New Jersey

It seemed that South Brunswick was walking into a den of ravenous lions desperate for information on how to use and deliver an individualized assessment program. Fortunately, we were able to find a room that could accommodate the group.

But the message was clear that day: Many educators were no longer willing to assess youngsters on useless, predetermined matters that have no application to what is being taught and emphasized in classrooms.

ABOUT SOUTH BRUNSWICK TOWNSHIP...

South Brunswick is a community halfway between New York City and Philadelphia, halfway between Princeton and Rutgers Universities, halfway between Trenton, New Jersey, and New Brunswick, New Jersey. It is populated by the scientists and engineers who work in the large "high tech" industries along Route 1 and by the technicians and truck drivers who support these industries. There are students who come from $400,000 homes, and there are those who reside in trailer parks along the highway. The population is approximately 9 percent African-American and about 19 percent Asian-American. We estimate that students speak more than 35 languages in our schools.

In Search of An Alternative

South Brunswick Township administrators and teachers have long felt the same frustrations regarding assessments available to measure the accomplishments of young learners. We were finding that prepackaged tests did not compliment our whole language/developmentally appropriate curriculum. Children were being assessed on irrelevant matters, thus setting the majority of youngsters up for failure. We were tired of apologizing for test results that we knew were inaccurately reporting a child's progress to parents. The music and the dance were not the same.

Several years ago South Brunswick early childhood educators and administrators formed a committee to discuss and "brainstorm" an alternative assessment for young learners. I am a full-day kindergarten teacher at Constable School in Kendall Park, New Jersey, which is part of South Brunswick Township, and I was one of the teachers who formed this group.

Our main objective was to develop an assessment tool that was complimentary to our whole language and hands-on approach to instruction. We decided that because children learn on an individual basis we needed an assessment tool that would be a reflection of the individual. We also wanted a system that would help us better communicate student progress to parents and other teachers, and one from which we could build school and community accountability.

After much research and discussion, we decided to start our alternative assessment venture by developing a portfolio system to assess the literacy progress of every child in kindergarten through second grade.

Committee members discussed the type of data that we would like to collect in the portfolio. We wanted information that would help us to challenge and measure students' growth as accomplished learners. We devised a list somewhat similar to the following, which is the list we use today.

☐ **Self-Portrait** (artwork)

☐ **Interview with the Child** (includes questions about literacy interests and attitudes)

☐ **Interview with the Parent** (includes questions about literacy attitudes)

☐ **Concept About Print Test** (activity that helps assess children's strategies for making sense of print, based on the scale in Portfolio Reproducible 4.3)

☐ **Word Awareness Writing Activity** (spelling activity developed by researcher J. Richard Gentry)

☐ **Sight Word List** (words come from those used in storybooks and texts that we use frequently)

☐ **Reading Sample**

☐ **Writing Sample**

☐ **Class Record** (attendance, evaluations of any type)

☐ **Story Retelling**

☐ **Optional Forms** (See Portfolio Reproducibles 4.1. - 4.6 for more specifics.)

Field-Testing and Revising the Components

Once we determined data to be collected in the portfolio, we gave early childhood teachers packets of the assessment materials they would need to collect this data. We also gave them one red expandable folder per student to serve as portfolio holders.

We asked the teachers to critique the assessment materials with two specific criteria in mind. First, are the materials useful? And then second, are the materials assessing what we are indeed teaching? During this trial process, we made many deletions and additions to the portfolio in response to field-testing feedback. We also began to talk more about assessment with each other

and with administrators – and even more important, we found ourselves using the same assessment language!

We began recognizing readiness in assessment as well. In other words, we determined that not all components should be regularly assessed every school year. (See Portfolio Reproducible 4.1 for suggested times.)

Another important thing that we found out early in our portfolio use is that it is not necessary to collect the same information on all children. For example, a particular child may not be ready for the Word Awareness Writing Activity (WA-WA). That in itself is valuable information. As a classroom teacher, who best knows the ability of that child at that particular moment, I can make

the teacher decision not to administer the WA-WA at that time.

Word Awareness Writing Activity (WAWA)

I would like to elaborate on the WAWA for a moment. It is the portfolio

We were tired of apologizing for test results that we knew were inaccurately reporting a child's progress to parents. The music and the dance were not the same.

component that I feel is most helpful in determining my students growth and develop-

STARTING YOUR OWN EARLY CHILDHOOD PORTFOLIOS?

1. Give plenty of thought to exactly what you are looking for.

2. Discuss materials and strategies to be used with colleagues.

3. Establish a common language that all can understand.

4. Be patient. Let a comfort level build with time.

5. Student portfolios require many hours of classroom time. Don't feel guilty about how much time it takes. There are only so many hours in a day. You may have to reorganize your schedule.

6. Administrative support is a must. Educate your principal.

7. Enthusiasm spreads, so spread it.

8. If something isn't working, it's OK to change it.

9. If you don't understand something about the portfolio process, find someone who does.

10. Team up with a colleague. Misery loves company.

ment. The WAWA is a developmental word-awareness and writing activity adapted from *You Can Analyze Developmental Spelling – and Here's How to Do It!* by J. Richard Gentry, (Early Years, May, 1985).

Some teachers prefer to give the WAWA on a one-on-one basis. Others choose to give it in small groups or once in a whole group situation. Given a choice, I'd rather use the one-on-one method. When children are working at different rates, I feel it is unfair to hurry children along or have them wait for others to catch up.

WAWA is administered something like this: The classroom teacher is given a list of 12 words (an optional list is also provided). The teacher says a word on the list and asks the child to write down what letters he or she hears in the word. The teacher encourages the child to say the words to oneself and write down the letters he or she hears. Once the child has written all 12 words, the teacher analyzes the list to determine the child's development stage in spelling.

There are five stages: Precommunicative, Semiphonetic, Phonetic, Transitional, and Correct.

❶Precommunicative spelling is the scribble stage. In this stage, the child writes/spells in random fashion.

❷Semiphonetic spelling stresses mostly beginning sounds.

❸In phonetic spelling, the child becomes aware of beginning sounds, ending sounds, and some vowel sounds.

❹The transitional stage shows the child getting much closer to the final stage.

❺In the correct stage (the final stage), the child demonstrates an understanding of beginning and ending sounds, along with proper vowel placement.

As a kindergarten teacher, I notice many children becoming empowered by this writing experience. If a child hasn't started the inventive spelling process, this activity usually sparks and motivates him or her to do so. Starting with the children who are at the semiphonetic stage on up, I hear comments like, "This is fun!" and "Can we do it again?" This activity also assists children in working independently and feeling good about themselves as readers and writers.

Developing Rating Scales

Many of the components in our portfolios required

some type of rating scale, or scoring rubric. Developing such a scale became our next step.

We wanted to ensure that we developed a highly reliable one, so we worked closely with Educational Testing Service (ETS) of Princeton, New Jersey, in this endeavor. Our cooperative effort resulted in the K-2 Reading Scale currently used by South Brunswick teachers to determine the "development of children's strategies for making sense of print." Portfolio Reproducible 4.2 provides the actual scale. The scale has proven to have a 95 percent inter-rater reliability, of which South Brunswick is extremely proud.

Our school district continues to work with ETS, which collects various data throughout the country regarding student portfolios and continues to look for ways to heighten uniformity and accountability in the area of individualized assessment.

Introducing Portfolios to Parents

Once we had defined, field-tested, and revised our portfolio components as well as a scoring rubric, it was time to officially use portfolios in the classroom and to introduce them to parents. At the next series of parent-teacher conferences, we sat down with parents and explained the components of the portfolio. We told them that the portfolio will follow their child through the second grade and that the classroom teacher will be using it at parent-teacher conferences.

The reception was extremely positive, especially as time went on. Parents soon discovered that the literacy portfolio supports what South Brunswick believes about young children, that they learn best in a developmentally appropriate environment that offers suitable age appropriate materials and tasks.

Today, parents are introduced to the portfolio even before their child has entered kindergarten. During our kindergarten orientation for parents, the red portfolio is presented and explained to each parent.

Integrating Portfolios into The Classroom

The one question I get asked most often from colleagues is, "How do you manage the use of the portfolio in the classroom?" Along with, "The concept in theory sounds great, but does it

We discovered early in our portfolio use that it is not necessary to collect the same information on all children.

really work?" I would like to briefly explain how I integrate the use of portfolios into my early childhood classroom.

Child-Centered Environment

First of all, environment

is extremely important. When you walk into the classroom what do you see? Is the classroom child-centered or teacher-directed? Are materials easily accessible to the children, or does the teacher dole out the materials? Are materials displayed for youngsters use on low shelves, or are materials kept behind locked doors?

You want to set up a classroom that is conductive to independent thinking, problem solving, and self-instruction. Youngsters have positive, self-worth when they know the classroom belongs to them, and they take on a special ownership for the housekeeping and safekeeping of materials. Students have supremacy in this type of environment.

Three Management Techniques

Within such a classroom environment, I currently use three management techniques in the classroom for instruction and individualized assessment. Here is how they work.

❶ Teacher-Directed, Timed Centers:

Divide the children into equal groups. Provide the same number of centers as groups. Example: If you have 20 students, you may want to have five centers with four children in each group. The teacher times the activities so each group attends each center for the same amount of time. When the time is up, the teacher signals for closure and then directs each group to the next center, until five rota-

tions are completed. One of the centers may be an assessment activity, such as a self- portrait or child interview.

❷ Child-Directed, Time Centers:

This works the same as the previous type except each child is given the opportunity to make choices and prioritize what activity he or she wishes to go to first. After the allotted time, the child decides where to go next, provided there is a space for him or her and that the child has not already been to that center or activity.

❸ Child-Selected, Timed Centers:

This is my personal favorite and the one I use most often. Using this technique, the child is left to make most of his

or her own decisions about both center selection and time. The first thing you need to do is decide a manageable allotment of students and centers for your classroom. It is very important to keep in mind that you will need more than enough spaces to accommodate all the children in the class so that freedom of choice is possible. A significant amount of time must also be allotted. In my classroom, center time runs anywhere from one and one-half to two hours. During this two-hour block of time, children also will encounter "must do" centers. The "must do" centers are almost always teacher- or adult-guided. It is here at the "must do" centers that you will most likely find a portfolio activity taking place, such as preparing writing samples or retelling stories. At the "must do" center, the teacher will pull children as space becomes available. The teacher may or may not see all the children in one day. In this case, you may plan the same activity for the next day or until you have collected the necessary data on each child.

Conclusion

It has been an honor and a pleasure to have had the opportunity to share "my story" with you. If you have any questions or comments, please don't hesitate to contact me. Early childhood educators are special people who are all striving for the same end result, the best education possible for young learners. ◆

Billy Age: 5
Pre Self-portrait
Sept 92

This chart is attached to the front of each red,
expandable folder that makes up a student portfolio.

Student's Name_____ School_____

Teacher's Name _____ Date of Entrance_____

	Pre K	Beg K	Mid K	End K	Beg 1	Mid 1	End 1	Beg 2	Mid 2	End 2
1. Self-Portrait	★	★		★	★		★	★		★
2. Interview with the Child		★			★			★		
3. Interview with the Parent	★	★			★			★		
4. Concept About Print Test		★		★						
5. Word Awareness Writing Activity (WAWA)				★	★		★			
6. Sight Word List				★	★	★	★			
7. Reading Sample				★	★	★		★	★	
8. Writing Sample		★		★	★		★	★		★
9. Class Record			★			★			★	
10. Story Retelling	★	★	★	★	★	★	★	★	★	★
11. Optional Forms										

★ = Time periods this assessment is done.

K-2 READING/WRITING SCALE

Development of Children's Strategies for Making Sense of Print

1 EARLY EMERGENT

Displays an awareness of some conventions of writing, such as awareness of front and back of books and distinctions between print and pictures. Sees the construction of meaning from text as "magical" or exterior to the print. While the child may be interested in the contents of book, there is as yet little apparent attention to turning written marks into language. Is beginning to notice environmental print.

2 ADVANCED EMERGENT

Engages in pretend reading and writing. Uses reading-like ways that clearly approximate book language. Demonstrates a sense of the story being "read." Uses picture clues and recalls storyline. May draw upon predictable language patterns in anticipating (and recalling) the story. Attempts to use letters in writing, sometimes in random or scribble fashion.

3 EARLY BEGINNING READER

Attempts to "really read." Indicates beginning sense of one-to-one correspondence and concept of words. Predicts actively in new material, using syntax and storyline. Establishes small, stable sight vocabulary. Displays initial awareness of beginning and ending sounds, especially in invented spelling.

4 ADVANCED BEGINNING READER

Starts to draw on major cue systems: self-corrects or identifies words through use of letter-sound patterns, sense of story, or syntax. Reading may be laborious especially with new material; new readings require considerable effort and some support. Writing and spelling reveal awareness of letter patterns and conventions of writing, such as capitalization and full stops.

5 EARLY INDEPENDENT READER

Handles familiar material on own, but still needs some support with unfamiliar material. Figures out words and self-corrects by drawing on a combination of letter-sound relationships, word structure, storyline, and syntax. Strategies of re-reading or of guessing from larger chunks of texts are becoming well established. Has large, stable sight vocabulary. Understands conventions of writing.

6 ADVANCED INDEPENDENT READER

Reads independently, using multiple strategies flexibly. Monitors and self-corrects for meaning. Can read and understand most material when the content is appropriate. Conventions of writing and spelling are — for the most part — under control.

Scoring:
NA = Not Applicable
Points 0-6

Note 1: The scale focuses on development of children's strategies for making sense of print. Evidence concerning children's strategies and knowledge about print may be revealed in both their reading and writing activities.

Note 2: The scale does not attempt to rate children's interests or attitudes regarding reading, nor does it attempt to summarize what literature may mean to the child. Such aspects of children's literacy development are summarized in other forms.

Rating scale developed by South Brunswick, New Jersey, teachers and Educational Testing Service staff, January 1991.

Interview with Child

Name _____ Date _____

1. What are your favorite things to do at home? _____

_____

2. Do you have your own books at home? _____

_____

3. What is your favorite book? _____

_____

4. Do other people at home like to read? What do they read? _____

_____

5. Who reads to you at home? _____

Parent/Guardian Interview

Dear Parents or Guardians,

Your input is invaluable in helping us develop a program for your child. Would you please take some time to answer these questions and return the form to me by _____ ? Thank you!

Sincerely,

Child's Name _____ Parent/Guardian's Name _____ Date _____

1. What are your child's special interests and strengths? _____

_____

_____

2. What are the types of reading and writing activities your child enjoys? _____

_____

_____

3. What else would you like me to know about your child? _____

_____

_____

Word Awareness Writing Activity

This activity may be done with the whole class, small groups, or individually.

1. Introduce the task by saying something like: "I'd like you to try to write some words that I will say. Even if you are not sure about what letters to use, go ahead and try." Because the task could be threatening, reassure the children that you do not expect them to know the correct spelling of the words.

2. Give each child a piece of paper (lined or unlined) and ask the children to put their name at the top. To help yourself decipher kindergartner's answers, you might ask them to fold their papers and write the first word at the top, the next word just underneath, and so on, moving on to the other side when there's no room at the bottom.

3. Provide some guidance by demonstrating the activity with a practice word. "Let's try a word together. Let's write the word *rat*. *The rat ate some cheese.* What letter do you hear at the beginning of *rat*? What other letters might be needed?" Whatever way you choose to introduce the task, it is important to support all answers. This is not a spelling test – we are trying to understand what children are thinking and are not concerned with their getting the right answers.

4. Dictate the rest of the words by using each in the sentence given. You may repeat each word as often as necessary. If a child seems overwhelmed and upset, you may excuse him or her from the activity.

1. **bed**	It's time to go to **bed.**	7. **feet**	My **feet** hurt.
2. **truck**	I see a dump **truck**.	8. **shopping**	**Shopping** at the mall is fun.
3. **letter**	The **letter** is in the mailbox.	9. **monster**	The **monster** is scary.
4. **bumpy**	The road is **bumpy**.	10. **raced**	The car **raced** down the road.
5. **dress**	I bought a new **dress**.	11. **boat**	I rode in a **boat.**
6. **jail**	The thief went to **jail**.	12. **hide**	Let's play **hide** and seek.

5. See body of article for directions for scoring.

Sample Sight Word List

Name _____ Date _____

LIST A Practice Word the	LIST B Practice Word is	LIST C Practice Word me
I	it	a
and	like	up
are	some	said
here	in	dark
be	you	away
for	cow	this
with	go	am
car	went	they
Mother	see	big
get	to	what
jump	sleep	can
dog	at	there
school	play	look
not	yes	on
ball	stop	bat
___ / 15	___ / 15	___ / 15

Reading Sample • Instructions

Establish a relaxed atmosphere. Ask students to read aloud as if they were reading along. Remind them: "When you're reading and come to something you don't know, do whatever you would do if you were reading all by yourself...as if I weren't here." Students must also know before they begin reading that when they are finished, they will be asked about the passage.

1. Procedure for Taking a Running Record (For Emergent Readers)

❖ Select material from trade books. (Use a known book to determine how well the child makes use of strategies that have been taught. Use an unknown book to determine the child's ability to integrate strategies independently.)

❖ Make a copy of the text selection and mark the miscues on it.
A Running Record is a way of looking more closely at what a young child is thinking and doing as he or she reads. When analyzing a running record, we are looking for growth in the following areas:
  • directional rules
  • one-to-one correspondence
  • use of visual cues (pictures, letters, words)
  • reading for meaning
  • use of reading strategies to self-correct miscues.

2. Procedure for Taking a Miscue Analysis (For Independent Readers)

❖ Choose selections from basal reading textbooks or from leveled reading inventory passages. The reading material must be unknown to the reader. The use of longer texts of approximately 150 words will produce more accurate information.

❖ Have the child begin reading a passage that is at least one level below his or her current reading level. Continue reading at successively higher levels as long as the child can read independently.

❖ When analyzing a reader's miscues, we must consider the nature as well as the number of miscues. Check reading for such characteristics as:
  • using preceding context to make predictions
  • making miscues that do not make sense
  • correcting miscues that do not make sense
  • achieving a balance in the use of the syntactic, semantic, and graphophonic cue systems.

❖ Please keep in mind that the purpose of a miscue analysis is to determine what strategies a child is using while reading. The reading inventories should be used as general guidelines and not to establish instructional reading levels.

Running Record/Miscue Coding System
For Reading and Writing Samples

1. **Substitution:**   Write substitution above the text.

2. **Omission:**   Circle word omitted.

3. **Insertion:**   Draw a caret mark (**∧**) and write word above it.

4. **Self-Correction:**   Write **sc** next to the corrected word.

5. **Repetition:**   Draw a line backward over the repeated words
                                  (beginning with the last word said).
                                  Write **R** and a number for each repetition.

6. **Word Reversal:**   (Example: was/ for *saw.* Draw line through word as shown.)

7. **Ignores Punctuation:**   Circle punctuation. (•)

8. **Teacher Assists with Word:** Write **T** above word.

9. **Teacher Prompt:**   Write **P** above the word.

10. **Teacher Says, "Try that Again:"**   Write **TTA** above the word.

Class Record

Does The Child . . .

Class List:	attend in large and small groups?		interact in large and small groups?		retell a story?		choose to read?		write willingly?	
	Fall	Spring	Fall	Spring	Fall	Spring	Fall	Spring	Fall	Spring

Directions For Story Retelling

What is it?

Retelling is a procedure by which a child recalls or reconstructs the important elements of a story. This can be done orally, or pictorially, or in writing.

Why use it?

Retelling helps to determine the reader's ability to comprehend text and stories, sense of story structure, and language complexity.

How to do it:

1. A retelling may be based on a book read by the child alone or one read to the child. Books selected should have good plot structures that make the storylines easy to follow and, therefore, easy to retell.

   If the teacher will be reading the text aloud, the material should be above the child's independent reading level, as children are generally able to more easily comprehend material read to them.

2. Tell children before reading or listening to the selection that they will be asked to retell it.

3. For the purposes of the portfolio retelling, it is very important for the story to be read from beginning to end without discussion.

4. For the purposes of assessment, it is crucial to allow the child to retell the stories without teacher prompts. The teacher should instruct the child to close the book before beginning the retelling.

5. Use the "Story Retelling Assessment Form." Put a check mark in the "Includes" column to indicate each story element the child retells unprompted. (Portfolio Reproducible 4.11).

6. Once a child has completed the retelling, you may elicit more detail and information. Put a check mark in the "Includes After Prompt" column for each item you must prompt.

Story Retelling Assessment Sheet

Child's Name _____ Grade _____ Date _____

Teacher _____ Book Title: _____ Author: _____

| ❏ **Story was read to child**
❏ **Child read alone** | ***Text Difficulty:***
❏ High Predictability
❏ Moderate Predictability
❏ Advanced Predictability | ***Response:***
❏ Oral Retelling
❏ Pictorial Retelling (Attached)
❏ Written Retelling (Attached) |

Story Structure	*Includes*	*After Prompt*	*Comments:*
Setting/Characters Starts retelling at beginning of story			
Names main character(s)			
Names other character(s)			
Tells when story happened			
Tells where story happened			
Theme Identifies goal or problem			
Plot/Events			
Includes all major events			
Tells events in sensible order			
Resolution Tells how problem was solved or goal was met			

Evaluative Comments:

Reader Reflections

Insights: _____

_____

_____

_____

_____

_____

Actions for Our School (District) to Consider: _____

_____

_____

_____

_____

_____

_____

_____

A Jump Ahead: Living with the KERA Portfolio Assessment

I live in a small town in central Kentucky (we call it the Bluegrass region) and teach English and chair the department in a small high school there. Although we laugh and say that you can't get to Danville from anywhere else because there is no interstate, passenger railway, or bus service in the town, Danville has other things going for it; for example, its sense of history as seen in its old homes and wide, shady streets; its downtown shopping area where one can still buy a cup of coffee for a nickel; and its schools.

I grew up here, went to the same high school in which I now teach — and have been teaching for the last 18 years — and I take a great deal of pride in the fact that although we are outside of the mainstream of big city life, at Danville High School, we manage to keep up, and sometimes even get one jump ahead.

Recently, our local newspaper printed an article that declared: "Danville Students Strong in Writing, Weak in Science." The article referred to the new assessment mandated by the Kentucky Educational Reform Act (KERA) —

VIRGINIA BILES

English Teacher, Department Chair
Danville High School
Danville, Kentucky

in particular, to its prescribed use of writing portfolios and on-demand writing samples. Well, we can't be good in everything, but we are good in writing. And here's the important news: We didn't get good by doing nothing!

What did we do?

We Started with Process Writing

First, we got involved in a small way in the process approach to writing early on, while the rest of the country, except for small pockets in the San Francisco Bay area and New Hampshire, were still working under the old paradigms. While working on my master's degree at the University of New Hampshire, I was randomly assigned to process-writing pioneer Donald Murray and became one of his "disciples." When I moved back to Kentucky, the "process approach" came to Danville. Then in 1989, I wrote a pilot school-writing grant that was funded by the Kentucky Writing Program. With the help of that grant, we trained all of our English department in the process approach to writing, and we were on our way.

Next, we began thinking of a way to save some of the really good writing our students were doing. What a shame, we reasoned, to return their writing folders at the end of the year, all that hard but excellent work, and then see it dumped in a trash can in the hall. More importantly, we reasoned, a sampling of a student's writing could help his or her next year's teacher understand the strengths and weaknesses of the writer and allow the teacher to work from there. No more reinventing the wheel every year. Thus the "showcase portfolio" concept was born.

We asked students at the end of the year to choose from their writing folders a narrative, a sample of writing to memorize, a story or a poem, two pieces of transactive writing, and a "best piece" with rationale. Then we asked them to write a letter to the reviewer, discussing their growth as a writer.

One student wrote: "My writing has developed in many ways this year. I could easily tell that when we recently revised some of the writing from back in the fall. My writing has changed as well as my views of what I wrote about."

Another said, "I have learned through the last year how to write more intelligently, and I have tried to write to the best of my ability. I have enjoyed being able to tell how much my writing has improved after going through the writing process."

And Then Came KERA

In July 1990 the Kentucky Educational Reform Act became effective. KERA mandates (along with site-based decision making and cooperative learning) assessment procedures to determine the level of each school's performance. The act requires that every child in the fourth, eighth, and twelfth grades produce a portfolio of material they have written, to write a sample to a given prompt, and to take a NAEP (National Assessment of Educational Progress)-like test. Based on scores for these activities in 1992-93, the schools were given a baseline assessment score; then they were assigned a threshold score that they will be required to reach by 1995. Schools that do not make the required progress will receive sanctions; while schools that accomplish their threshold score will receive bonuses. Our goal of improving student writing now had the proverbial carrot/stick motivation.

We moved into KERA portfolios with relative ease – after all, we were already in the portfolio business. The KERA portfolio was a bit different from our own "showcase" portfolio, but generally not anything we couldn't handle. It required a personal narrative; a short story, poem, or play/script; three pieces of writing that would achieve any one or more of various given purposes; and a letter to the reviewer in which the student reflected on the pieces in the portfolio and analyzed himself or herself as a writer.

However, not *every-thing* went smoothly. Most of the English teachers were committed to producing quality writing, but we all thought that we were leaving out too much of our curriculum – a great deal of literature – to get in the required writing. For example, I teach American literature and I got only as far as the "modern" writers, Hemingway, Faulkner, and Steinbeck. As much as I had read the theory in the literature and heard it in conferences, I could not totally convince my colleagues, and myself, that "less is more." Furthermore, we were not totally in agreement with KERA's scoring rubric and benchmarks, but we put aside our individual differences to strive for validity in scoring our portfolios.

Also, our students did not take the portfolio development seriously until our principal appealed to the school board to make a completed portfolio a requirement for graduation.

The biggest problem, however, came not from the writings from the English classes but from the two required writings from other curriculum areas. Students had little to put in as evidence of writing in other curriculum areas: some notes, answers to questions, an occasional essay or paper – generally undocumented.

The portfolios were scored (one to five points per prescribed standard) and then classified on the basis of novice, apprentice, proficient, and distin-guished. (See Portfolio Reproducible 5.1). When the scoring was completed, approximately 36 percent of our seniors had scored in the novice range and another 36 percent in the apprentice. While we were not unhappy with the

What a shame, we thought, to return students' writing folders at the end of the year, all that hard but excellent work, and then see it dumped into a trash can in the hall.

scores, we realized that to improve student writing all of the teachers at Danville High would have to be involved. Hence, Writing Across the Curriculum (WAC).

Next Step: Writing Across The Curriculum

The State Department of Education was on the same wave length we were: its Kentucky Writing Program funded model school writing-across-the-curriculum grants. I asked for volun-

Teachers understood that the writing portfolios were just that — writing portfolios, and not English portfolios.

teers from our faculty who would be interested in receiving training during the summer and the next school year, and then wrote a model-school grant. Because the idea behind the grant was that one school in a district would become a model school and at the end of the year disseminate information to the other schools in the district, I named the program "Spreading the Word."

We were awarded $20,000 to train a WAC team and to fund the program for one year, and our district agreed to give me three hours release time each day, including my planning period, to serve as on-site writing resource-teacher.

Then the fun, and work, really began. Sonia Cohen, a consultant from Louisville, Kentucky, spent two days with us, training 11 teachers from social studies, math, science, art, health, business, and special education departments in writing across the curriculum. This involved all of the aspects of the process approach to writing as well as writing to learn. The teachers were particularly receptive because our new assessment tool — the portfolio — was really driving the curriculum, and they understood that the writing portfolios were just that — WRITING portfolios, and not English portfolios. Their responses showed their enthusiasm: "I'm ready for school to begin (for once)!" Some were eager to "Spread the Word" to other faculty members, particularly to members of their own departments: "Once we have tried some of the strate-gies, maybe we can report the results, somehow, to the rest of the faculty."

Following the training, the teachers went into their classrooms full of ideas for implementing writing across the curriculum. We also returned to school feeling that we were a team — a Writing Across the Curriculum team. We were all in this together.

The students caught on pretty quickly that something was up. "Why should we write in math? Or science? Or art?" they argued.

"Because when you can write about a subject, that knowledge becomes truly yours," the teachers responded. "And we can tell whether you really do understand the subject!" And write they did! In all subjects.

Meanwhile, the training continued: Two more full days and then six two-hour after-school collegial meetings. We shared successes and discussed how to improve strategies; we learned about methods of publishing, telecommunicating, and revising and editing; and we wrote and shared our writings. The enthusiasm continued although the team members reported exhaustion ("I can't get it all done!") from the multiple demands of KERA. Comments included: "I am becoming more relaxed when doing writing things with my classes," "The sharing of ideas between teachers was most useful." "It's great to have time to share ideas, to discuss failures and successes."

Several teachers attended conferences dealing with writing across the curriculum and the use of technology in writing. We invited our area resource teacher from the Kentucky Writing Project to meet with us, and we attended in-service programs that featured other resource teachers from the state.

In the spring, we invited parents to visit the classrooms and see writing across the curriculum in progress. Before introducing the program, we asked them to remember a time they had to write in school and how they felt about it. They then shared their responses.

Only 30 responded to our invitation, not as many as we would have liked, but those who came responded favorably. Said one parent: "The emphasis on writing in all subject areas is wonderful. Writing not only augments the students' learning in each subject area, but it also improves their thought processes. Another parent added: "I especially enjoyed the actual writing; then group sharing; and the long, lost memories that both evoked."

Because many parents work, we also invited parents to an open house the same night. At the open house, team members shared samples of student work both completed and in progress. About 30 more parents came by for a look at what we were doing.

We wanted the entire community to know what we were accomplishing, so we saw to it that the school newspaper, *The Log*, and the community newspaper, *The Advocate Messenger*, both wrote articles about our program and our progress.

Results of Our Efforts

As portfolio scoring-time drew near (March 1993), Don Turner, the assistant superintendent, wrote an

Our new assessment tool — the portfolio — was really driving the curriculum.

Extended School Services (ESS) grant for portfolio improvement. Six teachers, three of whom were from the

Spreading the Word team, tutored five students each, three hours per week for six weeks. The idea behind the grant was to focus on those seniors who were writing at an apprentice level but who had the possibility of raising their scores to a proficient level. About 15 seniors and 15 juniors showed up for the twice weekly sessions. Students were excited about attending the writing sessions in the afternoons, and as one teacher said, "This is what teaching is all about."

As March closed in, the computers reached overload as students hustled to finish papers and teachers jostled for computer time to take classes to the lab. As the papers from the "other curriculum areas" began to come in to the English teachers, who had the responsibility of overseeing the compilation of the portfolios, we began to see progress – real progress – and we were optimistic that this year's portfolios would be better than last.

We did not know how much better until the scoring was completed and the scores validated. Novice portfolios which constituted 36 percent in 1992, were down to 9 percent in 1993; apprentice portfolios went from 36 percent to 44 percent; proficient, from 23 percent to 39 percent; and distinguished, from 6 percent to 8 percent.

According to Mr. Turner, who presented the findings, the emphasis on writing was accomplishing what it set out to do. Students were writing in all areas, and writing well. Superintendent Bill Grimes wrote in a newsletter to the teachers: "Our district's emphasis on writing, along with grants from the Kentucky Writing Program and ESS programs are paying dividends in the quality of our students' writings."

More importantly, I believe, students are enjoying writing and learning a communication skill that will be invaluable to them throughout their lives.

What Next?

We do not expect the going to be easy from here on. The scores next year will probably not reflect as big a shift as the 1993 scores. The money will not be available from the state department to continue funding the grant even on a smaller scale; therefore, any writing money will have to come from local funds. Although I have had some teachers express an interest in receiving training next year, many are stressed and stretched to the limit with other demands of KERA.

If the progress continues, and I am confident it will, it will be because our teachers believe in helping our students be the best they can be and because our school system understands the value of the first goal of KERA: Students will be able to communicate effectively. ◆

KERA* DESCRIPTORS OF WRITING PERFORMANCE LEVELS

Novice

The novice writer demonstrates a limited awareness of both the audience and purpose. The ideas expressed either ramble or are weakly organized. The writer includes only limited or unrelated details. The novice shows rudimentary understanding of correct and varied sentence structure and wording. Mechanical errors may be disproportionate to the length and complexity of the piece.

Apprentice

At the apprentice level, the writer shows an attempt to establish and maintain a purpose and to communicate with the audience. This writer demonstrates a logical focus of thoughts, and the ideas developed by the writer may include some personal reflection. Details supporting the main point(s) are unelaborated or repetitious. Simplistic sentence structure and language also characterize the apprentice performance level. Mechanical errors may be present; however, they do not interfere with communication.

Proficient

The proficient writer demonstrates the ability to present a fully-developed, focused piece of writing that communicates ideas clearly. In addition, the ideas that are communicated show elaboration and analysis. This writer also includes relevant details that support the main point(s). Sentence structure and word choice contribute to the effectiveness of the writing. Few mechanical errors are evident relative to the length and complexity of the piece.

Distinguished

At this performance level, the writer develops ideas with insight and perception. The writer organizes thoughts with care and precision and, furthermore, supports the focus with elaborated and pertinent details. Both sentence structure and language enhance the overall effectiveness of the writing. At the distinguished level, control of mechanics is clearly evident.

*Kentucky Educational Reform Act

ADVICE FOR IMPROVING PORTFOLIO ACHIEVEMENT

❶ **Start small; show progress.** Don't try to involve every teacher in your school. Instead, try to involve those who are really interested. Teachers who are lukewarm or hostile about getting involved in a project like this can undermine the morale of the group.

❷ **Explore state funding.** If grant opportunities are available, write a grant for a writing program, a writing across the curriculum program, or a portfolio program; if state funded summer workshops are available, attend them. Use state resource-teachers if they are available.

❸ **READ, READ, READ.** Read your National Council of Teachers of English journals, books on the subject, anything and everything you can get your hands on. If you have funds available, start a professional collection and encourage your teachers to read also.

❹ **Build a collegial support group from your teachers.** If your teachers can support each other, they can see each other through any rough times – and there will be some!

❺ **Find a consultant who not only knows his/her business but who also can establish the necessary rapport with the teachers.** This will do much to start the teachers toward the collegial support group.

❻ **Treat your teachers like professionals.** Try to get away from school when you have some meetings and when you score portfolios. Provide them with the materials they need to do their jobs. For example, a three-hole punch does wonders for building morale!

❼ **Keep the public informed.** Great PR means funds for your program.

❽ **Get your administration involved.** If your principal and your superintendent believe in what you are doing, they will give you the moral support and, we would hope, the financial support you need.

❾ **Attend conferences.** If you can find out what others in other sections of the country are doing, you can stand on their shoulders.

❿ **Involve parents.** They are, for the most part, interested in how their sons and daughters are scoring. Invite them to come to school to see your program and to see the completed portfolios.

Insights: _____

_____

_____

_____

_____

_____

Actions for Our School (District) to Consider: _____

_____

_____

_____

_____

_____

_____

_____

_____

ASSESSING
A Teleproductions Course

6

In northeast Ohio, about halfway between Akron and Youngstown, lies the small city of Ravenna. It is an old town that is just about the same size it was at the start of the Civil War. Ravenna is the county seat and thus the center of local government.

The 950 or so students in grades nine through 12 who attend Ravenna High School are part of the 3,400 young people who make up the Ravenna City School District. The student population very much reflects the economic make-up of the community. About half of our students are enrolled in the free lunch program, and many of our students' families are on various government assistance programs.

Ravenna is not a wealthy community. We are in the midst of another money crunch, and the school system will once again be asking the community to pass a levy that will raise property taxes. Three years ago, we were in the same type of bind, and it took several tries at the polls to pass the levy. I would venture to say that Ravenna is typical of today's small, struggling communities.

Around 1987, when finances were not quite as tight and money was earmarked for developing technology use in the classroom, administrators from Ravenna High purchased some teleproductions equipment and asked me to create an electives course in teleproductions. My name is Terry Kekic, and I have been teaching two teleproductions classes at Ravenna, along with other technology and social studies courses, every semester since.

TERRY KEKIC

Teleproductions Teacher
Ravenna High School
Ravenna, Ohio

Before the teleproductions course started, I outlined the traditional type of instructional plans for it. After a few weeks, however, I began to see that "traditional instruction" was not going to work. There was much that we wanted to do that did not fit into the lecture, followed by pencil-and-paper test.

For one thing, teachers in the building started to understand what we were able to do with our facilities and began to ask students in our two classes to videotape classroom lectures and demonstrations for them. This work was giving students excellent, hands-on practice, but the formal class was falling apart. Students were not always in class, but instead, out of the room on jobs that staff had asked us to do. The old way of grading with tests and other paperwork was not meeting our needs. I investigated the possibility of making this course pass-fail, but administrators, sensitive to college recruiters' preference for letter grades, rejected the idea. So, off I went on my travels through assessmentland to find a system that would allow me to reasonably assign letter grades to my students' progress.

This is the story of that trip that has yet to be finished, if indeed, it is possible or preferable to have it end. So far, the journey appears to fall into three phases.

Phase One

In the very first years of the course, I tried to keep the traditional manner of grading by working with students from a textbook and indeed giving written tests from the text on a regular basis. For hands-on experience, which is crucial in a teleproductions course, I organized projects or productions that involved the entire class, such as historical newscasts in which the students did research on an historic event and then incorporated their findings into the form of a late night news show.

Here was a course I could evaluate without any trouble, I thought. In theory, at least, that was true, but theory never did work well in my teleproductions classes. As I explained earlier, teachers throughout the building had my students performing various videotaping jobs for them. Because of these jobs, it seemed like we never had the entire class in the same room at the same time. At least not very often. Textbook lessons, tests, and even parts of the class projects were frequently postponed. Yet, I was not at all upset that the students were out of the room working on jobs because that meant students were solving teleproductions problems themselves, and hence involved in important learning. That seemed to me like the type of learning that should take place.

I began to encourage these independent projects and to show students ways to enhance them. But the new question became: How do I grade this type of work? I just assigned grades based on the quality of the students' work. The grades were really high because I would not accept any work that did not meet high standards. C or D work would never leave our room. I would not permit that to happen. Finished work was our calling card and lots of people saw it. The work had to be good.

The flaw in this system was that not all students had the same opportunities to perform jobs that had the same level of difficulty. There were some jobs that while necessary, were not jobs that required a lot of advanced skills. Then, too, some of the more challenging jobs had to be taped in the evenings when some students worked and so were not able to take part. To fill these gaps, I decided to assign jobs in our lab that refined skills such as camera work or graphics creation. This worked well, but there were many times that these assignments had to wait because required equipment was being used by a student performing a larger job.

I gave grades for all these activities, but did not feel secure about it. The grades seemed to be based on a lot of nebulous guidelines.

About this time, I began to have students collect their work on one or more (if necessary) videotapes. You could say I was beginning to have students develop video portfolios. These portfolios let me sit down with a student and review his or her work as a whole, noting progression and skill development.

The type of work in each portfolio differed greatly. No two students were doing the same things. So once again, I found it difficult to assign grades. Eventually, I developed a list of specific skills that I expected each student to demonstrate in his or her portfolio by the end of the semester. These included skills in camera work, audio work, video composition, and editing (see Portfolio Reproducible 6.1). The student and I would refer to this sheet each time we reviewed his or her portfolio.

Phase Two

The 1992-93 school year saw me change from an up-in-the-front-of-the-room teacher, if indeed I ever was one, to what I called an assign-ment editor. There were no more textbook lectures and tests. I would assign real jobs to students, and they would gather whatever resources they needed—including student power, technical equipment, and knowledge—to do the jobs.

By assessing their own progress, students became shareholders in their own destiny.

Some of the jobs were very simple and straightforward and could be done with a single student and no production equipment, such as researching famous birthdays and preparing scripts on the information for use on a *Raven-*

na *High School Morning News* show. Others were very involved projects, like producing the school's video yearbook, which requires a lot of equipment and several students working over the entire school year.

Once again, students kept all of their coursework, simple projects as well as complex ones, in a video portfolio. From time to time, each student and I would evaluate this portfolio. We used project assessment-sheets (which I continually revised to suit new types of projects) as well as the original skills checklist to help us assess the work. (See Portfolio Reproducibles 6.2–6.4.)

It was important that students had a role in their own evaluation. By assessing their own progress, students became shareholders in their own destiny. And it was only after receiving ample student reflection that I would eventually determine a letter grade to put on a report card (even then I was uncomfortable doing so).

During assessment talks, I also asked students to evaluate the course itself. I took great pains to ensure that they felt all comments were welcome. And they truly were. There is no doubt in my mind that the students' ideas about the course have been a big part of the changes that have taken place over the years.

I spoke to parents as well about the course. Several parents told me that at the start of the year, their children felt somewhat uncomfort- able with my method of not telling them what to do. I had only expressed my expectations of them in the most general terms. They were not used to that approach and did not know how to take it. It took time to understand that they needed to solve their own problems, that I would assist them on their quest, but not spoon-feed them the an- swers. But, parents said, after students discovered that they could indeed muster whatever re- sources were needed to solve the problems pre- sented by a project, they felt very good about themselves and the whole process.

And they deserved to. Our accomplishments for the year included these quality teleproduc- tions: *Ravenna High* *School Morning News, Marching Band High- lights, Football High- lights, Christmas Con- cert, Ravenna Hall of Fame Inductions, Na- tional Honor Society In- ductions, Spring Sing, Senior Awards Presenta- tions, Graduation Exer- cises,* and *Video Year- book* as well as selected girls' and boys' basketball games, and middle and elementary school plays and concerts.

Late in the 1992-93 school term, I met with my two classes for several days and talked about the type of projects students worked on during the past year. I asked them to rate the rela- tive difficulty of the differ- ent jobs they completed. For each project, I wanted to know the following.

◆ How hard or easy was it?

◆ How long should it take to complete it?

◆ How many people does it take to complete the job?

◆ What equipment did you need, and for how long?

◆ In short, I asked them to report on every task they finished and what it took to finish them.

I decided I would use this information as the base of a new assessment program for next year, one that would increase students' opportunities to solve real-life problems and also help me feel comfortable about prescribing letter grades to their work.

Phase Three (The Future)

Next year, I plan to have students bid on different jobs. I will post several projects, ranging from the very simple to the most complex and diffi-cult, on a bulletin board. For every project posted, I will prepare a sheet that outlines what is required to complete it adequately, and I'll file the sheet in a box or drawer marked "Teleproductions Projects."

After reviewing the job listings and their requirements sheets, students interested in a specific project will round up a team of other interested students and bid for it. The bid will contain the following.

◆ number of days the bidder thinks he or she will take to complete the job

◆ names of students the bidder requests to work on the project (the bidder will lead the team)

◆ equipment needed to do the job

◆ unusual approaches or ideas he or she would like to incorporate into the job.

I will reserve the right to award the contract to any student I choose. In theory, I would like to make the award to the bidder who enters the most efficient bid, one that keeps amount of time and number of team members low. However, I need to reserve the right to award contracts to a student team that may not submit the lowest bid, but has some great ideas for the project, is more realistic about the time and student power needed to do the job, and/or is generally better suited for the job.

Included on each job sheet will be a point value that will reflect the difficulty of the job, based on the information students gave me last year about their projects. I will use these points to determine grades for students every quarter. I will review each student's video portfolio with him or her and together we will determine if the projects have met all of the requirements for achieving the assigned points. I am not sure how many points I will assign to each letter grade; I will work that out soon.

Conclusion

I will continue to tinker with the assessment methods I use in my class because I believe that any teacher who stops looking closely at what he or she is doing will start sliding back in teaching effectiveness. You must keep moving ahead to keep teaching fun and exciting. ◆

Skills Sheet for TV Production I & II

Code: TV I = TV Production I   A = Awareness   D = Development   U = Upgrading
        TV II = TV Production II   E = Exploration   M = Mastery

STUDENT/SUBJECT OBJECTIVES	TV I	TV II
The students will be able to:		
1. Identify basic television transmission and receiving methods	D, M	U
2. Summarize the history of TV broadcast media	D	M, U
3. Operate the basic television camera controls	E, D	M, U
4. Diagram the setup of camera shots	E, D	M, U
5. Demonstrate one-camera production techniques	E, D	M, U
6. Produce a two-camera television production	E, D	M, U
7. Identify the various types of microphones	D, M	U
8. Manipulate audio transmissions on the audio mixer	E, D	M, D
9. Demonstrate the adding of an audio track onto a pre-recorded videotape	E, D	M, U
10. Operate a spectrum analizer – pink noise generator	M	U
11. Determine the effectiveness of various lighting angles	A, E, D	M, U
12. Demonstrate different lighting temperatures and how they affect color quality	A, E, D	M, U
13. Differentiate between inset and assemble editing	E, D	M, U
14. Relate the differences between editing and A/B roll editing	A, E, D	M, U
15. Write a script for a five-minute television show	E, D	M, U
16. Modify an incorrect storyboard and match it to a prewritten script	E ,D	M, U
17. Explain and make crew assignments for an interview show	A, E, D	M, U
18. Demonstrate uses of a switcher/seg with a two-camera, one-VTR setup	A, E, D	M, U
19. Prepare a computer-generated title and visual effect for use in videotaping	E, D	M, U
20. Perform insert and assemble editing on a videotape editor	A, E, D	M, U
21. Produce a music video by inserting audio onto an edited videotape	E, D	M, U
22. Defend choices of equipment with regard to features and price (after assembling a simulated home-video system)	D	M, U
23. Become knowledgeable about copyright laws in the area of teleproductions.	A, E	D, M

Self-Evaluation Sheet • Editing Exercise

Directions: Circle the response that most accurately describes your reaction to each statement below.

1 = strongly agree   **2** = agree   **3** = neutral   **4** = disagree   **5** = strongly disagree

1. The exercise effectively uses nearly all of the worthwhile raw footage.	**1**	**2**	**3**	**4**	**5**
2. The exercise included some especially entertaining segments.	**1**	**2**	**3**	**4**	**5**
3. The pace of the program was maintained.	**1**	**2**	**3**	**4**	**5**
4. Editing technique effectively emphasized certain actions.	**1**	**2**	**3**	**4**	**5**
5. Editing technique was smooth; the movements looked natural.	**1**	**2**	**3**	**4**	**5**
6. Major flaws (jump cuts, glitches, clipped footage, etc.) were avoided.	**1**	**2**	**3**	**4**	**5**
7. The audio was technically adequate.	**1**	**2**	**3**	**4**	**5**
8. Narration enhanced the exercise.	**1**	**2**	**3**	**4**	**5**
9. Music was effectively used on the program.	**1**	**2**	**3**	**4**	**5**
10. The overall production was entertaining.	**1**	**2**	**3**	**4**	**5**

Additional Comments: _____

_____

Self-Evaluation Sheet • Lighting Exercise

Directions: Circle the response that most accurately describes your reaction to each statement below.

      1 = strongly agree   **2** = agree   **3** = neutral   **4** = disagree   **5** = strongly disagree

1. Various types of lighting were used in this exercise.	**1**	**2**	**3**	**4**	**5**
2. The tungsten lights helped provide accurate, vibrant color reproduction.	**1**	**2**	**3**	**4**	**5**
3. Lighting helped emphasize certain aspects of the subject.	**1**	**2**	**3**	**4**	**5**
4. In some cases, lighting provided a visual sense of texture.	**1**	**2**	**3**	**4**	**5**
5. Lighting was effectively used to establish "atmosphere."	**1**	**2**	**3**	**4**	**5**
6. Lighting definitely enhanced this production.	**1**	**2**	**3**	**4**	**5**

Additional Comments: _____

_____

_____

_____

_____

Self-Evaluation Sheet • Video Portrait

Directions: Circle the response that most accurately describes your reaction to each statement below.

1 = strongly agree   2 = agree   3 = neutral   4 = disagree   5 = strongly disagree

1. The tape successfully provided a comprehensive view of its subject.

        1   **2**   **3**   **4**   **5**

2. The tape presented the subject in an interesting manner.

        1   **2**   **3**   **4**   **5**

3. The shots were sensibly ordered.

        1   **2**   **3**   **4**   **5**

4. The camera work was competently done, avoiding major flaws (shakiness, fuzziness, sudden shifts, etc.).

        1   **2**   **3**   **4**   **5**

5. The shots were well composed (centered, balanced, no edges chopped, etc.).

        1   **2**   **3**   **4**   **5**

6. Camera movement (zooms, pans, tilts, and combination thereof) enhanced the video portrait.

        1   **2**   **3**   **4**   **5**

Additional Comments: _____

_____

_____

_____

Reader Reflections

Insights: _____

_____

_____

_____

_____

Actions for Our School (District) to Consider: _____

_____

_____

_____

_____

_____

_____

I was not at all upset
that the students were out of the room
working on jobs
because that meant students
were involved in important learning.

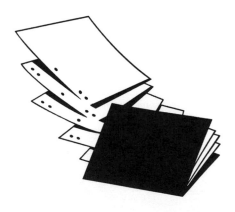

Selected Resources

Books

Belanoff, P., Dickson, M., eds. 1991. *Portfolios: Process and Product*. Portsmouth, N.H.: Heinemann, Boynton/Cook.

Myers, Miles. 1980. *A Procedure for Writing Assessment and Holistic Scoring*. Urbana, Ill.: National Council of Teachers of English.

Spandel, V., Stiggins, R.J. 1990. *Creating Writers*. New York: Longman.

Tierney, R., Carter, M., Desai, L.E. 1991. *Portfolio Assessment in the Reading-Writing Classroom*. Norwood, Mass.: Christopher Gordon Publishers.

Yancey, Kathleen Blake, ed. 1992. *Portfolios in the Writing Classroom*. Urbana, Ill.: National Council of Teachers of English.

Zemelman, S., Daniels, H. 1988. *A Community of Writers*. Portsmouth, N.H.: Heinemann.

Articles, Papers, and Reports

Campbell, J. 1992. Laser disk portfolios: Total child assessment. *Educational Leadership* 49(8), 69-70.

Coalition of Essential Schools. 1990. Performance and exhibitions: The demonstration of mastery. *Horace* 6(3), 1-12.

Educational Testing Service (ETS). 1989. The Student Writer: An Endangered Species? *Focus* 23. Princeton, N.J.: ETS.

Frazier, D., Paulsen, F.L. 1992. How portfolios motivate reluctant writers. *Educational Leadership* 49(8), 62-65.

Hansen, J. 1992. Literacy portfolios: Helping students know themselves. *Educational Leadership* 49(8), 66-68.

Hebert, E. 1992. Portfolios invite reflection—from students and staff. *Educational Leadership* 49(8), 58-61.

Hetterscheidt, J., Pott, L., Russell, K., Tchang, J. 1992. Using the computer as a reading portfolio. *Educational Leadership* 49(8), 73.

John, J. 1990. Literacy portfolios. DeKalb, Ill.: Northern Illinois University, Reading Clinic. (ERIC Document Reproduction Service No. ED 319 020)

Kansas State Board of Education. 1992. Assessment! Assessment! Assessment! Report by Kansas Quality Performance Accreditation. Topeka, Kans.

Knight, P. 1992. How I use portfolios in mathematics. *Educational Leadership* 49(8), 71-72.

McDonald, F., Kellogg, L. 1984. Monitoring students' academic and disciplinary progression. Paper presented at the annual meeting of the National Association of Secondary School Principals, Las Vegas, Nev. (ERIC Document Reproduction Service No. ED 247 649)

Meyer, C., Schuman, S., Angello, N. 1990. Aggregating Portfolio data. NWEA white paper. Lake Oswego, Oreg.: Northwest Evaluation Association (NWEA).

Mumme, J. 1989. Portfolios: A mathematics assessment alternative. Report of California Mathematics Project, Department of Mathematics, University of California, Santa Barbara, Calif.

Nelson, B., Sundberg, J. 1990. Portfolios. Paper presented at annual meeting of Iowa Educational Research and Evaluation Association, Des Moines, Iowa.

Paulsen, F.L., Paulsen, P., Meyer, C. 1991. What makes a portfolio a portfolio? *Educational Leadership* 48(5) 60-63.

Roettger, D., Szymczuk, M. 1990. Guide for developing student portfolios. Draft version. Material presented at the annual meeting of the Iowa Educational Research and Evaluation Association, Des Moines, Iowa.

Solomon, G. 1991. Electronic portfolios. *Electronic Learning* 12(5), 10.

Spady, W., Marshall, K. 1991. Beyond traditional outcome-based education. *Educational Leadership* 49(2), 67-72.

Valencia, S. 1990. A portfolio approach to classroom reading assessment: The whys, whats, and hows. *The Reading Teacher* 44 (January), 338-40.

Walters, J., Seidel, S. 1993. The design of portfolios for authentic assessment. Draft version. Material developed by Project Zero, Harvard Graduate School of Education, Boston.

Wolf, D. 1987. Opening up assessment. *Educational Leadership* 45(4), 24-29.

Wolf, D. 1989. Portfolio assessment: Sampling student work. *Educational Leadership* 46(7), 35-39.

Wolf, D., LeMahieu, P., Eresh, J. 1992. Good measure: Assessment as a tool for educational reform. *Educational Leadership* 49(8), 8-13.

Newsletters
Portfolio Assessment Newsletter. Five Centerpointe Drive, Suite 100, Lake Oswego, OR 97035.

Portfolio News. c/o San Dieguito Union High School District, 710 Encinitas Blvd., Encinitas, CA 92024

*Portfolio—The Newsletter of Arts Prope*l. Harvard Project Zero, 323 Longfellow Hall, Harvard Graduate School of Education, 13 Appian Way, Cambridge, MA 02138.

Notes:

_____

_____

_____

_____

_____

_____

Personal Resources

Individuals: _____   _____

_____   _____

_____   _____

_____   _____

_____   _____

_____   _____

_____   _____

Publications: _____   _____

_____   _____

_____   _____

_____   _____

_____   _____

Organizations: _____

Glossary

Assessment
Any systematic basis for making inferences about a student's learning progress.

Alternative Assessment
Usually, any assessment form other than standardized tests, commercial tests, worksheets, or textbook questions.

Authentic Assessment
An assessment that engages students in challenges that closely represent what they are likely to face as everyday workers and/or citizens. In other words, the context, purpose, audience, and constraints of an authentic assessment must connect in some way to real situations and problems. It could be in the form of a performance test, a set of observations, a set of open-ended questions, an exhibition, an interview, or a portfolio.

Descriptive Portfolio
A portfolio that demonstrates various skills a student can do, but does not attempt to evaluate the work according to set criteria. Material may be collected solely by the student or in collaboration with teacher(s) and/or parent(s).

Essential Outcome
Learning behavior or competency that a student must demonstrate before moving onto the next learning level or instructional unit.

Evaluative Portfolio
A portfolio in which every submission is subject to evaluative criteria. Material may be collected solely by the student or in collaboration with teacher(s) and/or parent(s).

Inter-Rater Reliability
A measurement concerned with how consistently a test is scored or behavior is rated by two examiners.

Literacy Portfolio
A record of learning that focuses on a student's literacy progress. The student and/or teacher may select work to go into the portfolio.

Outcome
Learning behavior or competency.

Performance-Based Assessment
A form of assessment that allows teachers to evaluate a student's skill by asking the student to perform tasks that require the skill. The student must perform with knowledge instead of merely recalling or recognizing other people's knowledge. A subset of authentic assessment.

Performance Standard
Defined levels of performance against which the performance of a student, school, or district is judged. One may choose to judge a student/school/district by local, national, or world standards of performance.

Portfolio
A record of learning that focuses on a student's work and often on his or her reflections on that work. Material may be collected by the student or in collaboration with teacher(s) and/or parent(s).

Reliability
The consistency of an assessment. If an assessment is not reliable, it is not always dependable.

Scoring Rubric
Guidelines for scoring a response (including the scale and description of the related criteria).

Showcase Portfolio
A record of learning that merely shows or celebrates work a student has done. The student selects what goes into to it. No evaluation takes place.

Units of Instruction
Major divisions or sections of content to be taught during the year that focus on one or more common objectives. Units usually focus on specific course topics or on a section of prescribed curriculum.

Writing Portfolio
A record of learning that focuses on a student's writing and (usually) his or her reflections on that writing. Writing samples may or may not represent various stages of the writing process, various writing genres, and/or various curriculum areas. The student and/or teacher may select the writing samples that go into the portfolio.

Notes:

_____

_____

_____

_____

_____

_____

The future is not some place we are going to,
but one we are creating.
The paths are not to be found, but made,
and the activity of making them changes
both the maker and the destination.

John Schaar
Researcher on School Change

THE

FAT
CAT

A DANISH FOLKTALE

by JACK KENT